ZULU LOVE LETTER

a screenplay

by BHEKIZIZWE PETERSON AND RAMADAN SULEMAN

ZULU LOVE LETTER

WITS UNIVERSITY PRESS

Wits University Press
1 Jan Smuts Avenue
Johannesburg
South Africa
http://witspress.wits.ac.za

Copyright © Bhekizizwe Petersen and Ramadan Suleman 2009

First published 2009

ISBN 978 186814 496 9 (Book)
978 186814 505 8 (Book with DVD)

All photographs taken by Tucha Basto. Tucha Basto is a Mozambican photographer who has exhibited widely under the name of Luis Basto. Copyright © Photographs Natives At Large.

Permission has been kindly granted to reprint the following reviews:
p. 25 – 'SA's most daring post-apartheid film yet' by Nasen Moodley – *Sunday Magazine, Sunday Tribune*, 7 August 2005.
p. 33 – 'No longer at ease' by Jyoti Mistry – *Lifestyle Magazine, Sunday Tribune,* 7 August 2005.
p. 34 – 'Silence speaks powerfully of hidden pain' by Moje Mokone – *The Sunday Independent*, 7 August 2005.

All rights reserved. No part of this publication may be reproduced, stored in a retrieval system, or transmitted in any form or by any means, electronic, mechanical, photocopying, recording or otherwise, without the express permission, in writing, of both the copyright holders and the publisher.

This material is based upon work supported financially by the National Research Foundation. Any opinion, findings and conclusions or recommendations expressed in this material are those of the authors and therefore the NRF does not accept any liability in regard thereto.

Edited by Pat Tucker
Cover design by Hothouse South Africa
Layout and design by Hothouse South Africa
Printed and bound by Creda Communications

CONTENTS

Foreword

Mbye Cham

Professor of Literature and Film in the Department of African Studies, Howard University

THERE WAS A MOMENT NOT SO LONG AGO WHEN FILMMAKERS and critics alike slapped the label 'weak script' on many an African film. Accurate or not, such observations draw attention to a fundamental element in filmmaking that convention, received or radical, posits as foundational in many respects. The idea that a film that works well for many emanates from a well thought out and written script, that a good film rests on the foundation of a good script, is a mantra embraced and championed by filmmakers who see the script – in all its diverse modes of being and specificities – as the template which guides the creation of a successful film.

Such imperatives have not been lost on many African filmmakers. In more recent times, in the arena of African filmmaking, we see significant shifts in matters of script, particularly as we witness a development now in film culture in Africa in which filmmakers, in partnership with oral artists, novelists, playwrights, scholars and trained scriptwriters/doctors conceive, develop and realise their projects. Examples from various parts of the continent abound and, in the case of South Africa in particular, the example of Ramadan Suleman, filmmaker, and Bhekizizwe Peterson, scholar/scriptwriter, stands out.

Working together within the context of their production company, Natives At Large, Suleman and Peterson have now collaborated on two feature film projects, *Fools* (1997), an adaptation of the short story by Njabulo Ndebele and *Zulu Love Letter* (2005), an original screenplay written by Peterson, and on a feature-length documentary on the life and art of Dumile Feni, *Zwelidumile* (2009). This partnership is taking place within a specific historical, cultural and political context and cinema practice that must be understood in order to appreciate better the achievement and significance of their films and, equally importantly, the publication of the screenplay of *Zulu Love Letter*.

It is always difficult, and perhaps ill advised, to generalise about and create rigid categories out of complex and constantly changing situations such as those in South African cinema. Moreover, in a foreword, it is also not possible to be comprehensive. However, for our purposes here we can identify certain key tendencies and orientations that intimate the limits and possibilities of South African film culture in the still unfolding post-apartheid moment.

The dismantling of formal apartheid in South Africa in the early 1990s spawned a number of moves and initiatives in all sectors of South African society which had as their express aim the doing away with the terrible legacy of apartheid and bringing about a new, democratic, non-racial South Africa.

In the area of cinema, in particular, and culture, in general, the years since 1994 have seen a flurry of activity accompanying, reflecting and driving a certain spirit of renewal, transformation, reconciliation, hope and confidence in a different future. This move to break with a racist past and bring about a renaissance, not just in South Africa, but on the entire continent, has become a prominent feature of South African scholarly, creative and popular discourse in the immediate post-apartheid moment. New institutions, both public and private, have been established, and older ones re-orientated to reinvigorate, promote, democratise and invest with a new mission many aspects of South African cultural practices that have always been valued as integral components of the struggle that brought formal apartheid to an end.

In the film sector, the lead taken by the government, along with private broadcasters and independent producers, distributors and entrepreneurs, to provide and facilitate resources, infrastructure and a general enabling environment has yielded a modest crop of new productions, new faces and a general film environment that is in the process of working out the contours and details of a new identity.

However, as welcome and encouraging as they may be on many counts, these moves are unfolding and struggling on a terrain that is still densely littered with the debris of apartheid. And it is also a contested terrain in which black filmmakers and others from historically disadvantaged populations are struggling to make inroads and make audible and visible their own voices and stories.

Filmmaking in South Africa is still dominated by white South Africans and, despite feeble challenges, American Hollywood products and models still dominate the country's mediascape, which has historically served, and continues to serve, as a location of choice as well as an outlet for many Western productions of feature films and commercials. The historically advantaged white filmmakers, most of whom have the advantage of better training and experience, continue to enjoy relatively easier access to resources, as rare and limited as these are for all. The relative absence of black filmmakers making films on 'black' subjects has produced a situation in which white filmmakers, at present, are the ones making the majority of films about black people and experiences.

Thematically, black criminal violence and the pathologies of township life seem to be a recurring feature of many recent films. The violence that has always been locked up in black township confines and, with the dismantling of apartheid-era controls, has suddenly found freer space to travel outside the townships, has provided much narrative material for filmmakers in South Africa in recent years.

One may wonder whether the current attraction in South African cinema to violence, crime and black pathologies in the post-apartheid era is a result of the 'afro-pessimism' of filmmakers and viewers. Some of these films simply pander to and exoticise violence and crime, while others engage this real life epidemic in ways that are critical and transformative.

South African cinema has yet to probe more profoundly and imaginatively the rich and troubled history, both distant and more recent, of this part of the continent. To be sure, there are films that allude to, reference and re-vision aspects of the apartheid past and their continuing import in the present. However, the history film as a genre, particularly films made from the points of view of the historically oppressed majority, is yet to emerge in South African film culture. Hollywood and Hollywood clones have thus far usurped the task. In the meanwhile, one has to look to a few films, in particular those that were inspired by the proceedings of the Truth and Reconciliation Commission, for narratives of memory and exorcism of the past. Also, linear realist modes of narration tend to dominate, and formal experimentation and forays beyond the conventions of received forms are still emerging.

It seems to me that in current South African film culture there is much activity but little movement forward. For the current generation of black filmmakers, in particular, the miniscule patch of space cleared by black pioneers has yet to be expanded and fertilised on a grander scale with new and different products. My sense is that to break out of the current confines and templates requires, among other things, investment in and access to resources, both public and private, that enable and promote creative independence and freedom. This would allow South African filmmakers, particularly black filmmakers, to begin to mine the rich fund of stories in South Africa waiting to be told, and to engage and reflect more profoundly and imaginatively on the crucial challenges and changes unfolding in the country.

For me, Ramadan Suleman's and Bhekizizwe Peterson's Natives At Large production partnership is an exemplary development in South African film practice and has thus far yielded much that is already the subject of critical engagement, celebration and commendation. In 1997 Ramadan Suleman splashed into South African film history with *Fools*, the first feature film directed by a black South African since Gibson Kente's 1976 *How Long*.

Zulu Love Letter, the company's second feature, engages the recent past in South African history in ways that are nuanced, complex, critical and compelling. Built on the foundation of a solid script that draws imaginatively from a Zulu construct, *'incwadi yothando'* [Zulu love letter], the film simultaneously mimics and transforms a long-established indigenous creative practice, the beadwork necklace, into a modern narrative device to structure and, indeed, propel an engaging personal and public story of the South African experience in a different medium. The skilful use of interludes (Peterson prefers this term to flashback) enables the film to capture and convey the nuances and complexities of state violence, memory, trauma, healing and restitution in the recent South African past; issues that are so much at the heart of the New South Africa in the process of becoming.

This creative deployment of indigenous constructs within the fabric of the film to talk about contemporary matters in a different way is, indeed, compelling and constitutes a significant step forward in the effort of filmmakers from various parts of the continent to develop a new film language, one that draws critically and in transformative ways on the rich repertoire of indigenous African structures, forms and styles. Little surprise that scholars and critics hail *Zulu Love Letter* as '... a thoroughly South African film ...'[1] '... that is in search of what a South African film is or should be'.[2]

The practice of publishing the script or screenplay of a film is yet to develop and take hold on a wide scale in African cinema. So, this publication of the script of *Zulu Love Letter*, along with the revealing and informative statements by the director and the scriptwriter, is quite significant. Particularly for student and young filmmakers, the pedagogic value of reading, studying and critically engaging with an acclaimed script is priceless. There is no doubt that, on a broader scale, scholars, critics, industry professionals and the general public will also welcome the availability of this script for their own purposes. It is my hope that more filmmakers will build on this commendable example of Natives At Large.

1 Jacobs, Sean. Critical comment on *Zulu Love Letter*. California Newsreel website. http://www.newsreel.org/nav/title.asp?tc=CN0179
2 Masilela, Ntongela. Critical comment on *Zulu Love Letter*. California Newsreel website. http://www.newsreel.org/nav/title.asp?tc=CN0179

▷ Detail of beads at Dineo's shrine

▽ Simanagaliso imagining Thandeka's wedding

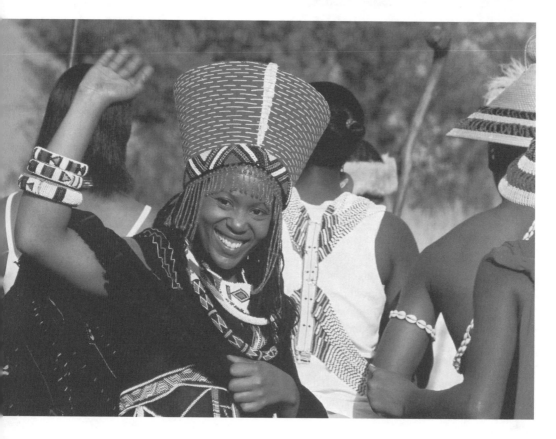

BEADWORKS AND VISUAL PRAISE POEMS

Anitra Nettleton

Professor of Art History, Wits School of Arts, University of the Witwatersrand, Johannesburg

FROM THE EARLIEST TIMES THE PEOPLE OF AFRICA have used beads as a means of dressing their bodies and thus expressing their status as well as their spiritual concerns. Not only did the Khoisan peoples of southern and East Africa make fine beads from ostrich eggshells, they also used other natural forms, such as bone and stone, to make body adornments. The ancient terracotta figures from Nok and other sites on the Jos Plateau in Nigeria are dressed in multiple beaded collars, arm and leg bands, and various forms of body coverings, which were probably beaded.

In southern Africa the speakers of Bantu languages who settled the subcontinent more than 2 000 years ago wore beads made of various materials. Locally produced beads made of metal, especially copper, but also gold, were highly prized, but were supplemented and eventually supplanted by glass beads. In about 1000 CE yellow and green glass barrel beads made their way into the African interior, via the East African trade. The beads, called 'beads of water' by the Venda and Pedi, were reserved for kings and leaders and were passed down through the generations, signifying the continuation of the lineage and the presence of the ancestors.

From the late 18th century small glass beads became available in increasing quantities via the European trade through the Cape and Delagoa Bay. Early on in the trade King Shaka maintained close control over the distribution of beads within the Zulu kingdom, so beads started out as prestige items, but in the Pondo Kingdom they constituted the value base of the economy until well into the 1830s and were available to all.

From the start Africans in the south of the continent favoured white glass seed beads, probably because the colour is related to spirituality and purity, and because white beads were used in contexts linked to the ancestral realm. The earliest beadwork known among Nguni speakers has a predominance of white beads, with a small number of colours distributed through it. This association of white beads with the spiritual realm carries through into contemporary beadwork, particularly that used by diviners and healers. However, as beads became more readily available both in the Eastern Cape and in KwaZulu-Natal, they also reflected changing fashions, with some colours being more popular than others at different times.

There have been varying accounts of the meaning of colours in Zulu beadwork, including that given by Princess Magogo, a daughter of Dinuzulu and mother of Mangosuthu Gatsha Buthelezi, to Jack Grossert, an inspector of education for black schools in the then Natal. According to Princess Magogo particular colours had meaning, but this significance always depended on the relationships between colours in the same sequence. Exactly how widely the meanings of colour would have spread within the Zulu kingdom is questionable; one can only demonstrate basic levels at which a common system of signs operated. Yet there have been consistent attempts to pin down such meanings, mostly by and for people looking into Zulu culture from the outside.

To appreciate the significance of beads in these contexts we need to shift attention from lexical definitions of the meanings of particular colours, or syntactical readings of the colours' arrangement in designs, to an understanding that beadwork signified many things beyond such confined symbols.

Most beadwork was at once public, because it was worn to be seen, and private, because it was made by an individual woman for someone of significance to her. Beadwork among the Xhosa was most commonly made for a young man by his girlfriend and for a married man by his mistress. In this sense it was a gift of love from one individual to another, and the messages contained in the beads spoke of these personal relations. Similarly, gifts of beadwork from Zulu maidens to their suitors would have conveyed aspects of the young woman's wishes, hopes and dreams. In many parts of South Africa mothers made beaded items for their daughters and aunts for their nieces. But beadwork was also used to create a range of garments used on ceremonial occasions such as marriage, the return of young men from seclusion in initiation, courtship rituals and first-fruit celebrations. In many of these ceremonies the wearers of the beads would dance, accompanied by music and song that invoked the ancestors and praised the living.

In the early 20th century beadwork styles came to be quite strongly differentiated along ethnic lines, and it was increasingly possible to differentiate not only Zulu from Tsonga or Ndebele beadwork, but also regional styles within Zulu and Xhosa beadwork. Beads could be worked to establish particular identities, as was the case with the extraordinary textured beadwork from the Maphamulo district, or that associated with the church of Isaiah Shembe. Tsonga diviners wear plain green, red and black wrapper-skirts with elaborate white beadwork, to mark their distinctive status. The way in which diviners from many parts of Africa adorn themselves with masses of beads also speaks to their connections with the spirit world and to their ability to sustain tradition in the face of the onslaught of modernity and foreign spirits.

Beadwork clothing appears to be so intrinsic to African imaging of the body that the first and only piece of clothing an infant traditionally wore was a string of beads around the waist. Beadwork has no life without the body that wears and animates it; as the body moves the light plays across and off the surface of the beads. Beads were used to cover leather garments; grass rings which covered the legs, arms and torsos of young women were completely encased in beads; and fertility figures were constructed out of beads to represent bodies covered in beads. In contemporary communities beadwork becomes a fashion accessory, something that enables all women, and some adventurous men, to make statements about the fact that they belong to an imaginary, contested, contemporary African community. African beadwork remains inspirational in imagining an African look and an African aesthetic that is historically rooted and yet modern.

Further reading:

Bedford, Emma (ed). 1993. *Ezakwantu: Beadwork from the Eastern Cape*. Cape Town: South African National Gallery.

Drewal, Henry John and Mason, John. 1998. *Beads, Body and Soul: Art and Light in the Yoruba Universe*. Los Angeles: UCLA, Fowler Museum of Cultural History.

Morris, Jean and Preston-Whyte, Eleanor. 1994. *Speaking with Beads: Zulu Arts from Southern Africa*. London: Thames and Hudson.

Nettleton, Anitra. 2007. 'Breaking Symmetries: Aesthetics and Bodies in Tsonga-Shangaan Beadwork'. In Nessa Leibhammer (ed). *Dunga Manzi, Stirring Waters: Tsonga and Shangaan Art from Southern Africa*. Johannesburg: Wits University Press and Johannesburg Art Gallery.

Pemberton, John III. 2008. *African Beaded Art: Power and Adornment*. Massachusetts: Northampton, Smith College Museum of Art.

Van Wyk, Gary. 2003. 'Illuminated Signs: Style and Meaning in the Beadwork of the Xhosa- and Zulu-speaking Peoples'. *African Arts* 36(3).

△ Thandeka and Simangaliso at play with the bead's project

LOVE, LOSS, MEMORY AND TRUTH

Jacqueline Maingard, PhD

Senior Lecturer in the Department of Drama: Theatre, Film, Television, University of Bristol

***ZULU LOVE LETTER* (2004) IS A BEAUTIFULLY EVOCATIVE** yet exceptionally painful film that confronts questions of truth and reconciliation in the South African context at the point at which the Truth and Reconciliation Commission (TRC) is beginning its proceedings.

The film tells its story through the primary characters of Thandeka (Pamela Nomvete), a journalist, who has personally experienced and witnessed apartheid atrocities, and Simangaliso (Mpumi Malatsi), her teenage daughter, who is deaf. It recreates the details of these atrocities through cinematic representations of Thandeka's memories, revealing their effects on Thandeka's life and psyche, as well as the consequences for Simangaliso and others around them.

I have described *Zulu Love Letter* elsewhere as 'an extraordinary film ... [that] creates a local narrative with national resonances; centralizes women and their experiences; engages an African aesthetics rooted in an African spirituality while sustaining an identifiable contemporary look and feel; draws the viewer into identification with its subject matter which extends its influence beyond entertainment and into the significance of historical and future realities'.[1]

In this analysis I will discuss *Zulu Love Letter*'s 'extraordinary' achievements in opening up new ways of (re)presenting traumatic memory in film. This is facilitated by the film's narrative and aesthetic choices, which position it outside the mainstream as less a classical film in the mode of 'Hollywood' convention, and more as an art film. Moreover, the fact that it espouses sensibilities rooted in an African context and portrays its debt to other African films, for example *Finyé* (*The Wind* 1982) and *Hyènes* (*Hyenas* 1992), also shifts its forms and functions beyond the conventions of classical cinema. In my earlier work on the film[2] I commented on the significance of its flashback sequences based on Thandeka's memories as well as the flashforward moments experienced by Simangaliso. In the present discussion I focus in detail on Thandeka's flashbacks, arguing that they are 'posttraumatic'.[3]

Some writers have grouped *Zulu Love Letter* with three other TRC-related fiction films, *Forgiveness* (2004), *In my Country* (2004) and *Red Dust* (2004), describing them as 'TRC films', which Lesley Marx identifies as a 'now-accepted genre'.[4] The notion of a 'genre' presupposes repeated codes and conventions, and a comparative approach suggests that this particular application to these films needs to be problematised.

While there are some similarities across all four films there are also major differences, not only in content and subject matter but also in formal aesthetics and styles. These TRC-related films were all produced at more or less the same time and may be seen as responses to social, political and cultural imperatives at the time, after the TRC's proceedings. While thematically they all refer to, or recreate, to lesser or greater degrees, aspects of the TRC proceedings, *Zulu Love Letter* does not directly represent them. It references the TRC, however, as a context in which many people have a stake. This is portrayed iconographically in the communal protest, with people carrying banners listing the names of their loved ones who have disappeared, as well as in the queues of people dressed in black, snaking through the township, waiting to register for the TRC.

On the township streets women, similarly in black, walk together carrying or leading goats intended for sacrificial slaughter. Dineo's sister bemoans the repeated recurrence of mourning ceremonies for those who have been assassinated and whose bodies have never been found. *Zulu Love Letter* goes even further, however, in that it extends a criticism of the TRC and the inability of its regulated, court-like proceedings to soothe the raw wounds of individuals and communities traumatised by apartheid atrocities. This is portrayed most explicitly in Thandeka's confrontation with the TRC councillor (Patrick Shai). When she scales his wall and forces her way through his guards, the passion of her emotions is pitched against his stand-off distance, in a microcosmic display of this incapacity.

THE STORY AND NARRATIVE STRUCTURE

Zulu Love Letter is primarily a story about a mother-daughter relationship – that between Thandeka and Simangaliso. The film intertwines two narrative strands; one in the film's present, located just before the TRC proceedings began (around 1996), the other representing the past. In the early 1980s Thandeka had witnessed the assassination of a young activist, Dineo, by an apartheid hit squad. She subsequently wrote about it for the *Weekly Mail* (later the *Mail & Guardian*), accompanied by a photograph of the event taken by her friend, Michael Peters.

Both of them were detained and tortured; Michael was killed and Thandeka survived. Thandeka was in the early stages of pregnancy at the time and Simangaliso is now deaf as a result of the beatings Thandeka received in detention. These two characters are pivotal to the plot, which revolves around Thandeka confronting her past and the personal shame she has carried since Dineo's assassination.

Communications between Thandeka and Simangaliso, now fourteen, have broken down. Thandeka has not learnt sign language and is embarrassed by this in public. Simangaliso, meanwhile, enjoys an easy relationship with her father, Moolla (Kurt Egelhof), separated from Thandeka, but still present in their lives. Simangaliso herself has special qualities, highlighted by the beautiful tapestry she is creating, incorporating found objects, beads, photographs, threads, ribbons and her own handwritten or drawn messages for her mother, father and grandparents. This is the 'love letter' of the title.

Thandeka's inability to come to terms with her past is given renewed emphasis by the call for people to register their intention to testify before the TRC. Dineo's mother, Me'Tau, approaches Thandeka to help her find her daughter's bones, to which she agrees. Thandeka accompanies her when she goes to register at the TRC. Meanwhile, however, Simangaliso needs Thandeka and needs explanations about Thandeka's former life, and this is a further challenge to Thandeka. The hit squad of three assassins who assassinated Dineo is under threat of exposure. Me'Tau tells Thandeka that she has visited one of the assassins four times.

After Thandeka visits the shop and home of this assassin with Me'Tau, the assassins begin to intimidate Thandeka. One of them searches her office and pushes a photograph of Michael under the door of her apartment. Later they orchestrate the apparently accidental death of Moolla in a motor accident. Simangaliso wanders the city streets alone, trying to get home after the accident and Thandeka searches for her in vain, finally finding her on her return home.

Me'Tau is also intimidated by an assassin, who parks his car opposite her house, watching her. She decides not to testify. Thandeka, Me'Tau, their families, friends and the TRC councillor who Thandeka has confronted earlier in the film, along with his supporters, attend a memorial ceremony at the farm where Thandeka and Michael were detained and where Michael was killed, in which they mourn their children and invite their spirits to return home. Subsequently, at Me'Tau's house, where participants add their gifts to the ceremony of remembrance conducted in Dineo's memory, Simangaliso and Thandeka present Simangaliso's 'love letter'.

By the end of the film, therefore, Me'Tau's need for resolution has been fulfilled sufficiently that she may no longer need nor want to testify. On the other hand, the intimidation to which she has been subjected could be the basis for testimony and, in the future beyond the end of the film, a character typified by Me'Tau may well testify, as one of a number of 'solutions' to her loss and the need to know. Similarly, Thandeka has achieved recognition of the value of her own 'story', a renewed commitment to Simangaliso, and to her relationship with her, as well as a new sense of self within the framework of the broader 'community'. But beyond the film's ending such a character may well choose also to testify.

FLASHBACKS

Zulu Love Letter is a complex 'treatise' on questions of truth. It argues that while the quest for truth plagues those who have been traumatised, 'truth' can never be discovered or revealed as a singular set of facts. Moreover, the TRC may have achieved a visibly communal/national form of excavating and even exorcising the atrocities of the apartheid past, but the multiple, repeated experiences of individual trauma, loss, grief and mourning need more than that. Words fail humanity at times like this. Transposed into film, realism and the restrictions of encoded conventional means fail to describe satisfactorily apartheid atrocities and the trauma left in their wake.

The flashback sequences in *Zulu Love Letter* engage the viewer in an edgy, modernist encounter with Thandeka's search for truth as well as the broader epistemological questions the film poses about truth per se. The repeated flashbacks to Dineo's assassination, woven into the plot from the first sequence in the film, are a key feature of the overall narrative structure, showing how Thandeka's memories of her traumatic political past constantly haunt her.

The six flashbacks, or 'interludes', as the writer, Bhekizizwe Peterson, prefers to describe them, partially interrupt the narrative flow. For example, in the opening sequence, Thandeka is found in her car, apparently in a coma. Whether she has blacked out because of alcohol or has tried to commit suicide is not entirely clear. In the ambulance the camera zooms very slowly into a close-up of her face. She has an oxygen mask over her mouth, her eyes are wide open and staring, the sound of her breathing dominates the sound track.

The image cuts to a fast-paced, fragmented sequence where we catch glimpses of newspaper posters, blurred movements on the street, a glimpse of the church building where Dineo was killed inter-cut with an anonymous camera protruding through a car window with the sound of the shutter clicking, all accompanied by political protest songs fading up and down on the soundtrack.

The presence of the camera highlights the significance of the photograph as document of the apartheid war that was fought on city and township streets, with both journalists and police making photographic archives in this way. At the level of the police, the camera acts metaphorically to signify both the 'taking' of activists' images with a camera and police snipers taking activists' lives by exchanging the camera for a gun.

Since we later see Michael in action photographing Dineo's assassination as well as her assassins, the camera at the car window offers a variety of ambiguous meanings. Later, we also see a photograph of Michael, an iconic reminder of the existence of police files on activists. Coming at the very outset of the film, then, this sequence has the effect of usefully establishing the period and context of Thandeka's story. Soon afterwards, in hospital, she has another flashback that, for the first time represents Dineo's assassination. The content of this particular flashback is repeated, with slight variations, at other times in the film, as we shall see.

In the light of the central place of these flashbacks/interludes in the film it is useful to consider how flashbacks have been used in film generally, the purposes they serve and how they function. As a starting point, Susan Hayward provides a helpful broad definition: '[a] narrative device used in film (as in literature) to go back in time to an earlier moment in a character's life and/or history, and to narrate that moment'.[5]

She takes this further by highlighting the subjective nature of flashbacks, asserting that they are 'a cinematic representation of memory and of history and, ultimately, of subjective truth'.[6] From this definition we can see that flashbacks act as a means of representing a character's subjective point of view. They thus 'narrate' both that point of view and the 'moment' or memory that they replicate cinematically.

In *Zulu Love Letter* we negotiate the content of Thandeka's memories, and the truths they may reveal, through Thandeka's eyes and, crucially, through her own subjective experience of her memories. Joshua Hirsch's discussion of flashbacks in Holocaust films is helpful in this context, primarily in the distinction he makes between 'classical flashbacks' and 'posttraumatic flashbacks'.[7] The former are more closely linked to classical realist films and the latter to Hirsch's notion of 'posttraumatic cinema', a cinema that is formally modernist, matching the subjective inability to pin down exactly the memory of the trauma experienced.

The 'classical flashback' is easily assimilated by the viewer, the film usually providing cues that there is about to be a flashback. Time is not disrupted and the shift from the primary narrative into the flashback and out of it again, back into the narrative stream, is seamless. 'Posttraumatic flashbacks', on the other hand, destabilise the viewer. They are tied into the character's subjectivity in ways that formally mirror her/his experience of the traumatic event. They are thus experiential, recreating the character's experience and, at the same time, also making possible the viewer's experiential witnessing of the event. This type of flashback has very strong resonance with the representation of Thandeka's posttraumatic memories in *Zulu Love Letter*.

Thandeka experiences flashbacks of different events that describe the past with which she needs to come to terms and with which she is imbricated. Having established the context of the times in the first, the second is a further flashback to Dineo's assassination, which the third repeats slightly differently. The fourth is a flashback to Michael's death at the farm. The fifth is, in effect, a conglomerate of flashbacks, including a sequence that shifts Thandeka's former positioning in her earlier memories, incorporating a different view of Dineo's assassination. The sixth flashes back to the cell where Thandeka was detained.

While each of these is significant in its own way, my primary focus is the interrelationship between the two different incarnations of Dineo's assassination in Thandeka's flashbacks: the first is the event she and Michael witness, presented initially in the second flashback and repeated in later flashbacks; the other is more like a dream in which the event is presented in a very different way; one that links Thandeka to it, as we shall see.

Like Hirsch's 'posttraumatic flashbacks' these 'interludes' are destabilising and shocking for the viewer, not only because of the formal properties of the images and sounds and the ways in which they are drawn together in a sequence, but also as a result of the timing in the broader narrative structure. The first and second flashbacks come within the first four minutes of the start of the film. At this point the viewer is still establishing the subject and content of the film and, specifically, wondering what has happened to Thandeka.

The loud, jarring, free-jazz music coming from her car's sound system over the discovery of her body is, in itself, quite a shocking opening. Although there is a 'classical' cue that the first flashback is about to occur, even if we did recognise it as such, its proximity to the start of the film prevents its assimilation. Thus, when the sound begins to shift as the lens slowly zooms into a tight close-up on Thandeka's face lying in hospital, rather than 'reading' it as a cue, we do not know what to expect. Just as we begin to register this uncertainty, we are catapulted into the frenzied, chaotic blurred images that characterise all the flashbacks.

The shift in sound seems to replicate the breathing of a person who is running and acts as an identificatory mechanism that reinforces Thandeka's point of view. With the camera on her face and the sound beginning over the image in the present, before cutting to the flashback imagery, it could also be the sound of her breathing into the oxygen mask. This breathing sound is aligned with the running that accompanies all the flashbacks of Dineo's assassination. In these flashbacks (with the exception of the last), Thandeka and Michael are running into the church, where they hide and from which they witness the killing, which Michael photographs.

Dineo is running away from the assassins' car and from the assassins themselves as all three close in on her and pin her against the wall. From the first flashback, therefore, the sound effects, alongside the images that visually replicate the events from Thandeka's point of view, draw us viscerally into the world of her traumatic memories. The other sound effect in the first flashback to the assassination is the ambulance siren that acts as a linking device between past and present. In this sense, the film replicates posttraumatic experience, where the 'victim' does not distinguish between the two; the past traumatic event maintains currency in the present.

The second flashback establishes the deep-seated roots of Thandeka's distress that explain everything that follows. This is the first view we have of Dineo's assassination. Strictly speaking, it is two flashbacks, in that towards the end of the sequence the image cuts back briefly to a close-up of Thandeka's face, before continuing. Past and present are elided, however, since the sound accompanying the flashback continues over this image of Thandeka in hospital.

The combined elements of the flashback establish a sequence of events leading to the assassination. Dineo and a young man are being chased by two men in a car. She is separated from her companion and becomes the single object of the chase. The car pulls up in the dust. She tries to escape between some houses but is cornered by the assassins. Meanwhile, Thandeka and Michael run into a building alongside, their footsteps clattering loudly on the soundtrack. It looks like the interior of a church, where they hide behind a wall while Michael takes pictures.

Dineo has her back to the wall (literally) and raises her fist in a power salute. One of the assassins points a gun at her head as she slides down the wall, silently mouthing the political slogan, *Amandla! Awethu!* [Power! To the people!]. This is where we momentarily cut to the image of Thandeka in hospital with the sound-over of the image now replicating a distant cry of *Amandla! Awethu!*. When the image cuts back to the flashback sequence we hear the sound of the gun going off, while the camera lingers on Thandeka's face, reinforcing her sense of horror. There is a slow fade to black as the flashback sequence ends.

The next flashback occurs about twenty-six minutes into the film, after Me'Tau, Dineo's mother, has been to see Thandeka at her workplace, asking her to find Dineo's remains. As she watches Me'Tau leave Thandeka has a short flashback that repeats some of the elements of Dineo's assassination that we have seen previously. On this occasion Dineo is running away from the car, which pulls up in the sand and one of the assassins climbs out and follows her. It re-uses images from the earlier flashback and, although it is truncated by comparison, ending with the dust from the car clouding the picture as the assassin follows Dineo, it resembles the earlier one closely enough for us to see it as a return to the same memory.

Within the first third of the film, therefore, we have already seen two separate, though closely matched, flashbacks to the killing. Another fifty minutes or so pass before Thandeka flashes back again to the event. This time the flashback is rendered in a more substantially complex way. Taken as a whole, it has three parts: the first is a repeated version of the assassination that matches the earlier two flashbacks; the second is a sequence at a roadblock; the third is a further flashback to the assassination, this time represented very differently, placing the killing in a complex sequence of events, where there is further blurring and fragmentation.

This is not only as an aesthetic device in sound and image, as in all the other flashbacks, but also bridges the boundaries of past and present. In these ways, the realities of Dineo's experience become more complex in themselves. Elsewhere I have described this flashback as a 'dream',[8] which its surreal qualities would seem to suggest. This is especially because it begins by repeating now familiar elements of the earlier flashbacks. This time we see Michael and Thandeka running into the church and crouching behind the wall at the window. Dineo is against the wall, her fist raised, the three assassins in front of her, the gun to her head. This short sequence ends on Thandeka's horrified look, from which the image cuts to black.

Rather than returning to a shot of Thandeka that is clearly in the present we enter the next section of this complex flashback, which segues from the dark screen of the last image to a torch flashing in the dark, signalling a roadblock. Thandeka is driving her car, with Simangaliso in the back seat. This is disturbing for the viewer. If it is the 1980s, Simangaliso would not be in the car. In the late 1990s white policemen would probably not have been manning a city road block, forcing black men to lie down and holding guns to their heads, unless, perhaps, it was a crime scene. If that were the case one would expect other motorists to be waved on rather than stopped as Thandeka is, her driver's licence checked, the car boot examined and torches flashed in Simangaliso's face.

While the roadblock scene is not in the same stylistic register as earlier flashbacks it still destabilises the viewer, not only because of its distressing content, but because it uses jump cuts. Neither sound nor image is distorted but because the shift between images is not seamless the sequence leaves the viewer uncertain. Since it is Thandeka's point of view that we follow, our experience matches hers, reinforcing identification with her subjectivity.

As she drives away, her headlights reveal glimpses of bodies lying face down, with police guns aimed at them. From Thandeka's point of view, the car swings very close to this horrific scene, the camera panning past it, the sound of police sirens over the image. The sirens, as in other flashbacks, act as a cue for Thandeka's flashback/dream represented in the next sequence (the third part of the flashback).

The image suddenly jumps to a different close-up view of Thandeka's terrified face, from the other side of the car, as distorted sound effects come up on the soundtrack and the image blurs like those in the other memory flashbacks. As she looks out of the window on one side a jump cut to the other side shows Me'Tau standing outside her house in the road shouting out Dineo's name as the image pans past, the camera positioned with the car. The loud, whirring sound of a helicopter dominates as an extreme top shot from the helicopter's perspective shows its light picking out the car.

The car stops suddenly and Dineo jumps out of the passenger door. This signals a major departure from the earlier flashbacks to Dineo's assassination. The image cuts back to Thandeka, now out of the car and shouting Dineo's name after her, mirroring Me'Tau's earlier action. Dineo runs into the frame, the low angle of the camera etching the white walls of the church and the cross on top against the dark night. She falls to the grass in front of the church, not onto sand, as before. As she looks back over her shoulder an assassin strides into the bottom edge of the frame. This time he is holding the gun in his left hand, not his right, as he was before. Dineo lifts herself up and begins to walk away as we hear the sound of two gunshots, not one. Thus, while the earlier flashbacks to the assassination are recognisably similar, here we have one of a completely different order, whose meanings I shall attempt to unravel.

The next few images cut between Thandeka and Dineo on their matching eyeline, a shared visual exchange that locks them together. In a close-up observational side shot Thandeka walks forward then stops, a look of shock and horror on her face, with the sound effect of a slowly fading heartbeat over the image. From Thandeka's point of view we look down at Dineo as she falls onto her back. She looks back at Thandeka, her gaze now directly at the camera. In this moment, Thandeka's memory/dream images expose the 'impossible history'[9] that she has carried within herself since she witnessed Dineo's assassination and how far she has become 'the symptom of a history that [she] cannot entirely possess'.[10]

In other words, by pushing the boundaries of her earlier 'posttraumatic flashbacks' this 'posttraumatic dream' provides Thandeka, and the viewer, with the symbolic illustration of the guilt and shame she has carried since the event. Not only did she witness the assassination, she could not/did not stop it. The handheld camera that searches the frames of the earlier flashbacks, extending beyond the action and returning to find it again, comes to rest in this intimate moment between Dineo and Thandeka.

The dream gives us, as viewers, the clue to the contours of her trauma and gives her the knowledge of herself that will enable her, finally, to take responsibility for herself and her life in the present. In other words, it acts as the therapeutic beginnings of 'working through' the trauma she has carried. In cinematic terms, the eyeline match between Dineo and Thandeka achieves more than this, however, because it is also a match with the viewer's eye-line. Thus, as she dies, Dineo is, in effect, also holding the viewer's gaze, positioned within Thandeka's subjectivity. In this way, the viewer stands in for Thandeka, whose bond with Dineo is, at once, both indelibly entrenched and replicated by/for the viewer. The viewer is thus never allowed the position of objective, observational witness, outside history.

This final rendition of the assassination and the two women's shared gaze is all the more powerful because in the flashback to Michael's death, just over forty minutes into the film, there is a similar construction of the gaze. In this sequence Thandeka walks alone among the trees on a farm she is visiting. Distortions of sound and image signal the flashback nature of the sequence. The image of Michael's face appears, gazing directly at the camera and thus, by extension, at the viewer. As the flashback develops, Michael is seen in a wheelchair, where he begins to have convulsions.

Two of the assassins are playing ball, the third is reading a magazine, none of them paying any attention to Michael's condition. Indeed, they are clearly passing time while awaiting his slow, torturous death. He looks to the side of the frame, in the direction of the assassins, his gaze directed at the camera and, therefore, at the viewer beyond. It dislocates the viewer from an observational comfort zone to one that interlaces him or her with the horrific events on screen. As we later discover, the farm is probably where Thandeka herself was held and the implication is that she may actually have witnessed Michael's assassination and death. The fire in the background and the barbeque where one of the assassins turns meat as Michael lies dead are a chilling reminder of other similar stories of apartheid atrocities.

SUBJECTIVE REPRESENTATIONS IN TRC-RELATED FILMS

A comparison of representations of posttraumatic memories and subjective interiorities between *Zulu Love Letter* and the other TRC-related films is useful here. In *Forgiveness* (2004), the film's chief protagonist is an apartheid assassin, Tertius Coetzee (Arnold Vosloo), and it is his subjectivity that the film represents. This is achieved through the viewer's privileged vision of his haunted moments of solitude in his hotel room. The camera is fixed on him in close-up as he repeatedly puts eye drops into his eye.

In a close-up shot of his face in the shower, the camera catches the light on the drops of water in slow motion, slowly dissolving and cutting between shots that reinforce the sense of his personal disturbance. On one occasion he wakes in the night and later falls asleep fitfully in front of the open window. He wakes again and jumps from the window and the following morning finds him at the tap in the yard outside, apparently flagellating himself with a rolled up piece of hosepipe, simulating his acts of violence against his 'victims'.

By focusing on Coetzee's interiority in these ways the film takes this fictional account outside the context of the TRC, containing its reach by individualising it. Coetzee is thus no longer perpetrator of apartheid atrocities but, in the developing account of his contact with the Grootboom family whose son and brother he killed, he becomes their saviour. This is evident from the outset, as Coetzee drives towards Paternoster, where the Grootboom family lives, a St Christopher medal dangling from the rear-view mirror.

Like the lone hero/anti-hero of the Western genre, Coetzee has centre stage and mythical status. His real purpose in the narrative, however, contains elements of the masochistic. Building on the scene where he flagellates himself with the hosepipe, ultimately he chooses to stay in Paternoster and to martyr himself, in the knowledge that he will be killed. While the Grootbooms are, by and large, represented in two-dimensional form, the film plots the course of Coetzee's personal trajectory and the resolution for his character equates with the film's resolution as a whole.

In my Country positions its two main characters, Anna Malan (Juliette Binoche) and Langston Whitfield (Samuel Jackson), as dual protagonists, who develop an inter-racial affair, while covering the proceedings of the TRC. The film is framed by Langston leaving his wife and child in the US to take up his commission in South Africa and returning to them at the end, which thus centralises his place in the story.

Anna is ascribed a unique level of interiority, however, with an occasional switch to a voice-over of her thoughts, drawn and adapted from Antjie Krog's poetic renditions in *Country of My Skull* (1998), on which the film is based. For example, on one occasion during the proceedings the camera focuses on her face and, as her gaze drifts off-frame and the ambient sound dims, signalling her subjective shift towards her internal thoughts, we hear her voice-over: 'In their Sunday best they come/mothers and wives/searching for a place to put their grief/truth has become a woman/everybody recognises her/and yet nobody knows her.'

While the film re-enacts aspects of actual cases brought before both the Human Rights Violations Committee and the Amnesty Committee, its chief engagement is with the two protagonists and their reactions to the TRC within the context of their developing relationship. By the end of the film, in the format of a classical resolution, each has returned to his/her partner and family.

Of the three TRC-related films apart from *Zulu Love Letter*, *Red Dust* (2004) incorporates memory flashbacks most fully, while containing them within a classical, conventional film mode. The flashbacks are linked to the character Alex Mpondo (Chiwetel Ejiofor) and develop as a growing narrative of his recall of the events leading up to the death of his comrade, Steve Sizela (Loyiso Gxwala). They begin as memory flashes, the first almost subliminal in its brevity. It takes place when Alex is swimming in a pool, the flashback signalled momentarily by his strokes going into slow motion, followed by a quick flash of Steve's bloody face.

Like the relationship between Thandeka and Dineo in *Zulu Love Letter*, represented by their shared gaze, the relationship between Alex and Steve in *Red Dust* is also represented by a gaze/'look'. At the end of the film, when Alex's recall is complete, he describes the last time he saw Steve, as his body was being dragged away. 'He gave me a look,' he says to his lawyer, Sarah Barcant (Hilary Swank), which he thinks sometimes was accusing and at others was a comradely recognition that they had made it and held out under torture, without giving anything away.

By the end of the film, through Alex's efforts, and his developing memories of the events leading to Steve's death, Steve's grave is unearthed. Their torturer, Dirk Hendricks (James Bartlett), whose amnesty application Alex is opposing, had buried Steve's body with the file dockets that implicate his superior, Piet Muller (Ian Roberts). Finally, as the narrative reaches its resolution, Alex withdraws his opposition to Hendricks's amnesty claim and Muller is arrested. The hint of a potential romance between Sarah and Alex is never realised and, at the end of the film, it is clear that Sarah intends to return to New York, while Alex's integrity as a former African National Congress cadre and now Member of Parliament is maintained.

In *Zulu Love Letter* Dineo's 'look' is not explained in words, but the film's exposition of Thandeka's life and the communal grief and mourning that culminates in the final memorial metaphorically resolve the need to recover the 'bones of the slain' and to 'breathe life into them' (the priest's biblical words, taken from Ezekiel). While the film concludes its narrative by ending at this point it is clear that, unlike in the other TRC-related films, there is no easy closure to the quest for truth and reconciliation and, indeed, no closure at all. Tragically, for 'victims' like Dineo, who are present only in memory, and who are otherwise silenced and voiceless, it is all too late in any event.

CONCLUSION

Zulu Love Letter's ending proposes that local rituals of remembrance that reinstate communal, familial and individual love and respect may provide a better means of long-lasting emotional support, alongside the public performances of truth and reconciliation orchestrated in the ambit of the TRC. This is certainly true for those who, like Thandeka, will always carry the memory and the pain, and Simangaliso, who embodies it and will always be marked by it.

Elsewhere, in the context of reflecting on the emerging contours of a national cinema in South Africa, I concluded that *Zulu Love Letter* 'strives to expose truth and reveals the impossibility of ever fully knowing it. Yet there have been terrible abuses of humanity exacted under apartheid that film is in a position to visualise on behalf of those who survive them. *Zulu Love Letter* has bravely created a new cinematic space for 'representing historical truths.'[11] In the same way that new film movements emerge at particular moments in history, *Zulu Love Letter* pushes the boundaries of films before it and makes leaps that hopefully the filmmakers themselves will continue to develop and others will seek to emulate and find the means to do so.

References

Caruth, C (ed). 1995. *Trauma: Explorations in Memory*. Baltimore: Johns Hopkins University Press.
Hayward, S. 2006. *Cinema Studies: The Key Concepts*, 3rd edition. London: Routledge.
Hirsch, J. 2004. *Afterimage: Film, Trauma and the Holocaust*. Philadelphia: Temple University Press.
Krog, A. 1998. *Country of my Skull*. London: Jonathan Cape.
Maingard, J. 2007. *South African National Cinema*. London and New York: Routledge.
Marx, L. 2006. ' "Cinema, Glamour, Atrocity": Narratives of Trauma'. *Social Dynamics* 32 (2), pp 22-49; reprinted in M Botha (comp). 2007. *Marginal Lives and Painful Pasts: South African Cinema after Apartheid*. Cape Town: Genugtig!.

1 Maingard, J. 2007. *South African National Cinema*. London and New York, pp 177-8.
2 Ibid, pp168-178.
3 Hirsch, J. 2004. *Afterimage: Film, Trauma and the Holocaust*. Philadelphia.
4 Marx, L. 2006.,' "Cinema, Glamour, Atrocity": Narratives of Trauma', *Social Dynamics* 32(2), p 49n 22. Apart from these fiction films, there are also a number of TRC-related documentary films including *Between Joyce and Remembrance* (2003), *The Gugulethu Seven* (2001), *Long Night's Journey into Day* (2000) and *We Never Give Up* (2002).
5 Hayward, S. 2006. *Cinema Studies: The Key Concepts*. London, p 153.
6 Ibid.
7 Hirsch 2004, op cit.
8 Maingard 2007, op cit, pp 173-5.
9 Caruth, C (ed). 1995. *Trauma: Explorations in Memory*, Baltimore, p 5; Hirsch 2004, op cit, p 92.
10 Caruth 1995, op cit, p 5.
11 Maingard 2007, op cit, p 178

WRITER'S STATEMENT

Trauma, art and healing

Bhekizizwe Peterson

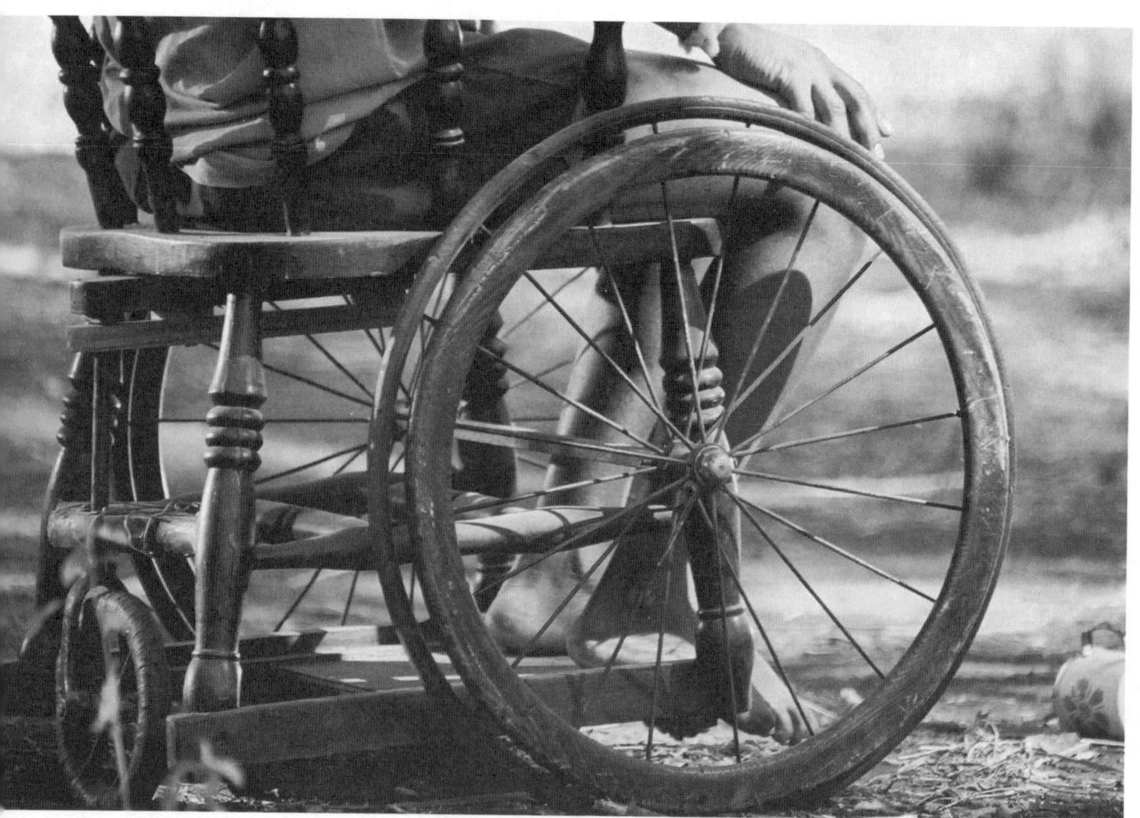

I STARTED WRITING *ZULU LOVE LETTER* IN ABOUT 1998 under the working title of *Until a Certain Time*. One of the buzzwords of the political landscape during this period was 'transition'. South Africa, we were told, was going through a 'transition' or was in a 'state of transition'. I was also struck by how 'state' tended to be used in two senses: to refer to a form of institutional governance and as a mental condition, 'the psyche of the nation'.[1]

It is not surprising that one of the imperatives of the new South African government was to foster a sense of national unity and nationhood among the disparate racial and social groups that inhabit the country. The notion of a 'rainbow nation' and the aspiration of reconciliation were extolled in pursuit of these admirable ideals. Both notions, however, were seriously flawed in a number of respects. Consistent with the continuing dominance of whiteness (that is, the reproduction of white cultural values, political assumptions and privileges as normative), the invocation of a nation that is 'united in its diversity' did not allow, even as an ideal, for any sustained and meaningful wrestling with the politics of race and inequality, both in the past and in the present.

What fascinated me was how to capture and challenge – on the level of theme, character and structure – the assumptions made about time and experience, forms of personal and social change, healing and redemption. The political changes were often glossed over as a 'miracle' and there was a feeling that 'in the fullness of time' things would resolve themselves and life would get better. The problem is that no one seemed to know the duration or content of a 'transition' nor of a 'government of national unity'. So, while political developments offered real reasons for hope, they also frequently came across as more adroit strategies of reinventing the status quo, now without the veneer of crass racism, oppression and exploitation, and under the remit of 'nation building'.

I was intrigued by what I suspected would be a much longer and more complicated historical and political condition than the idea of a 'transition' allowed for. I sensed a phase that is analogous to Antonio Gramsci's 'crisis of authority' or 'interregnum', where 'the crisis consists precisely in the fact that the old is dying and the new cannot be born; in this interregnum a great variety of morbid symptoms appear'.[2] The challenge, then, was how to capture in the theme and form of the film the sense of uncertainty, of the myriad tensions between past, present and future. I do not know whether we resolved this challenge successfully but we were clear that the narrative needed to explore concerns that were in danger of being ignored, repressed or glossed over because they went against the grain of the 'feel-good' mantras of the new dispensation. Not to do so was to abdicate the role of the arts in speaking the unsaid or unspeakable. Distressingly, then and now, many morbid symptoms attested to the convulsions of the state and the nation. Crime, corruption, violence against children and women, xenophobia and extreme racism are continuing ailments that everyone agrees about and regards as unacceptable.

However, it remains unclear how nation-building is to move beyond being merely an ideal if, as a society, we continue to deny and repress the many social problems and pathologies that are our inheritance from the past. In this regard two symptoms remain particularly stunning and inform the thematic ambit of *Zulu Love Letter*.

The first is the difficulty South Africans have in acknowledging and responding to the deep psychological and economic scars that are the result of a society structured on racial domination and exploitation. The second, which I suspect is partially provoked by the stubborn and unbearable weight of the first, are the attempts to create all forms of equivalences between the violence and brutality of apartheid and the humanity and conduct of black people, whether as individuals or as part of oppositional political groups.

Under the banners of whiteness we are reminded that black people and the resistance movements have *also* committed acts of 'criminality' and abuse of human rights. There are enough cases to validate such a position but they should not be used to recast the imperatives of, in particular, accountability and justice. Distressingly, even artists have been unable to avoid the impulse of disavowal. There are significant numbers of confessional testimonies, novels and films exploring these questions and, unfortunately, very few have been able to escape the strictures of whiteness in their accounts.

Even worse, the difficulties and imperatives of forgiveness are recast and turned into yet another trial of the compassion and humanity of those who have been offended and hurt. As far as reconciliation is concerned, there seems to be little appreciation that its pertinence far exceeds the boundaries of black and white relations. Individuals like Thandeka and Me'Tau need to come to terms with themselves and their experiences, relatives need to reconcile within families, relations between neighbours and communities need to be restored where these have been broken.

In a chapter entitled 'The Grey Zone', which tellingly evokes the interregnum, Primo Levi, reflecting on his experiences at Auschwitz, acknowledges that 'the network of human relationships inside the Lagers was not simple: it could not be reduced to the two blocks of victims and persecutors'. In a passionate attempt to understand the collaboration and 'uncomprehended aggression' of fellow inmates Levi offered a number of cautionary insights. Firstly, he suggests that, given that collaborators are untrustworthy, 'the best way is to burden them with guilt, cover them with blood ...' so their complicity will make it impossible for them 'to turn back'. Secondly, he avers that 'the harsher the oppression, the more wide spread among the oppressed is the willingness to collaborate with power'. He then adds that '... it is imprudent to hasten a moral judgement' because whatever 'the concurrent guilt of the individual' it 'must be clear that the greatest responsibility lies with the system, the very structure of the totalitarian state ...'

Levi also unequivocally rejects attempts to create equivalences, or, in his words, the

> exchange of role between oppressor and victim: I am not an expert of the unconscious and the mind's depths, but I do know that few people are experts in this sphere, and that these few are the most cautious; I do not know, and it does not interest me to know, whether in my depths there lurks a murderer, but I do know that I was a guiltless victim and I was not a murderer. I know that the murderers existed, not only in Germany, and still exist, retired or on active duty, and that to confuse them with their victims is a moral disease or an aesthetic affection or a sinister sign of complicity; above all, it is precious service rendered (intentionally or not) to the negators of truth.[3]

On the level of plot we were clear that we needed a narrative that would not be linear and resolved in the classical sense; that a loose, open-ended structure would probably be better suited to the kinds of questions we wanted to pose. Consequently, there are at least two ways in which you can approach the narrative-arch of the film.

Many viewers have tended, for obvious reasons, to read *Zulu Love Letter* as another 'cinematic take' on the Truth and Reconciliation Commission (TRC) in South Africa. Even though the film is set against the backdrop of the success of the first democratic elections and the launch of the TRC, for me the film is the story of two mothers in search of their daughters.

Thandeka Khumalo is challenged with mending her estranged relationship with her thirteen-year-old daughter, Simangaliso, who grew up with her grandparents because of Thandeka's career and political commitments. Tormented by a sense of guilt and grief that refuses to wane, Thandeka is battling to adjust to the changes around her. Her melancholy soul is compelled to confront her experiences of detention and torture when ghosts from the past reappear.

Me'Tau, the mother of Dineo, a young activist whose assassination Thandeka witnessed and reported, wants Thandeka to help her find Dineo's body so she can be given a fitting burial. For mourning to end and for healing to take place the psychic demons that haunt the present must be recognised and exorcised.

On the level of the life journeys of the characters there is a discernable movement from conflict to denouement: Thandeka and Simangaliso do narrow the gulf between them and Dineo is laid to rest in line with her mother's wishes. But as far as the larger socio-political questions are concerned, the unfinished and messy business of apartheid does not lend itself to any tidy solutions. The racial, gender and class inequalities and inequities remain intact, perpetrators are still free, victims are still in limbo, reparations are still under consideration and debate. Another attempt to achieve a free structure was in the use of what I prefer to call 'interludes' rather than flashbacks. The interludes, in Thandeka's case, are intended simultaneously to encapsulate and disrupt the coherence of time and the certitudes of experience and memory. Her recollections of Dineo's assassination, for instance, signal the unreliability of memory, the impact that trauma can have on the individual that leads to the inability to know fully or to articulate experiences of extreme violence and the belated insight that can come from witnessing or experiencing trauma. Whatever the case, Thandeka's recollections do not contest the murder of Dineo. They draw us into sensory experiences and knowledge that is often destabilised and erased by the valorisation of forensic facts.

On another level the fractured nature of the structure was intended to parallel Thandeka's psychic state. It is also my belief that violence is better narrated in oblique rather than direct ways: that instead of realism, more affect and effect is achieved by hinting at or postponing the moment of violence or by compelling viewers to complete the 'scene of violence', hopefully drawing on their personal fears and knowledge of suffering.

In contrast, Simangaliso's interludes are fantastical in their fusion of the real and imaginary, the past, present and future, and in their projections of her desires and creativity. Whereas her mother's interludes address brutality, Simangaliso's seek ways of avoiding violence, mourning and loss and, instead, will into being the promise of healing and love.

Both kinds of interludes, however, suggest, in their own manner, ways of dealing with the past and the interregnum.

As far as dealing with the complexities of mourning, anger and healing are concerned, the ills of the nation are not likely to be overcome if citizens are not granted the space and time to address their personal and localised anxieties in ways that are not necessarily consistent with or parallel to the initiatives and needs of the larger society. The fallacy is to assume that the nation (the body politic) experienced grief during the apartheid past, that such wrongs were acknowledged in processes such as the TRC, and, moreover, that with the modalities of democracy in place the nation is now in a position to overcome the pains of history. The challenge now, whiteness often intones, is to 'close the chapter on the past' and 'move on' if we are to achieve unity and the goals of the new dispensation. In many ways, such a position is the inverse of that of those, like Thandeka, who insist on upholding the ethics of mourning, whether it is through anger or the insistence on restorative justice.

The fact is that individuals do not always apprehend time as a neat and chronological sequence, nor do they attach the same significance to the relationship between time and experience or deal with trauma in the way societies would often prefer them to. For Thandeka, the fragments that serve as the mnemonic symbols of the past continue to manifest themselves in the present. The Toyota Corolla that is the mark of the apartheid snipers is confused with one parked in front of her flat when she, Simangaliso and Moola arrive. The women dressed in black are the embodied monuments to the missing and the dead.

For many among the lower classes poverty, discrimination and alienation continue, even though there has been a change in government. In short, survivors of trauma may find themselves caught up, in Lawrence Langer's brilliant formulation, in 'durational time' instead of 'chronological time'.[4] In such instances, the passage of time does not confer forgetting, closure or redemption. Faced with 'a past that will not pass',[5] survivors like Thandeka are called upon to confront the mental debris that 'speaks' – whether through silence (or the unspeakable), nightmares, hallucinations, guilt or anger – to their experiences of violence.

There is no easy walk to healing and not all paths begin with the official or legal interventions. People have embarked on journeys in search of self-preservation and restoration through reestablishing the appropriate relationships with the divine, ancestors, the land, self and community; through spiritual and material means that facilitate an anchored and wholesome existence.

The routes of African spirituality, ritual and art have been crucial in this respect. In practice, the distinction between ritual and art can be tenuous, given the reliance of both on symbolic performance and its evocation of, on the one hand, imbalance, fragmentation, pain and distress and, on the other hand, the different channels and forms of transcendence and convalescence. The mental and bodily manifestations of trauma are symbolically embodied and, hopefully, negotiated or, better still, negated through ritual therapy. Simangaliso's 'love letter' encapsulates the therapeutic role of the arts and their capacity to foster love and healing through memory-work. The film, as a product, is an extension of this idea. It is an attempt to commemorate publicly and interactively the violence of the past, keeping it alive in the communal consciousness in order to, in its own small way, also serve as a deterrent against a repetition of the history it engages. It is, ultimately, also a ceremony and tribute to victims and survivors.

△ Khulumani members during a break in filming

1 Rose, Jacqueline. 1998. *States of Fantasy*. London: Oxford: Clarendon Press, p 6-7.
2 Gramsci, Antonio. 1971. *Selections from the Prison Notebooks*. London: Lawrence and Wishart, p 275.
3 Levi, Primo. 1988. *The Drowned and the Saved*. London: Abacus, pp 22-33.
4 Langer, Lawrence. 1993. 'Memory's Time: Chronology and Duration in Holocaust Testimonies'. *Yale Journal of Criticism* 6 (2), pp 263-73. See also Langer, Lawrence. 1998. *Preempting the Holocaust*. New Haven: Yale University Press, pp 26-33.
5 Spiegel, Gabrielle M. 2002. 'Memory and History: Liturgical Time and Historical Time'. *History and Theory*. 41, p 159.

SA's most daring post-apartheid film yet

Nashen Moodley
FILM

FILM: Zulu Love Letter
Director: Ramadan Suleman
Starring: Pamela Nomvete, Mpumi Malatsi, Sophie Mgcina

RAMADAN Suleman's *Zulu Love Letter* is angry, serious and compelling cinema, uncompromised, unafraid and quite singular in the canon of South African post-apartheid cinema. Aesthetically and politically, it is, to my mind, the most daring film to have come out of post-1994 South Africa.

Suleman's superb first feature, 1997's *Fools*, is one of my favourite South African films. Like *Fools*, *Zulu Love Letter* is not a film that can be flirted with. It demands (and deserves) your complete attention. What is so exciting about *Zulu Love Letter* is that it is a quite successful attempt to subvert the formulas to which we have become accustomed.

The narrative is non-linear, the main character is often unlikeable, the dialogue is never simplistic, and the camera is always doing interesting things. It seems sometimes that the actors are baring their very souls. It is so close to the bone that it sometimes makes for uncomfortable viewing.

And that, of course, is *Zulu Love Letter*'s intention. It does not seek to comfort or placate, instead it unflinchingly looks at the heavy personal toll political struggle can take on people. And it suggests, strongly, that forgiveness is not always possible.

Zulu Love Letter revolves around Thandeka (Pamela Nomvete), a journalist in her 30s, who is grappling with a South Africa that is on the verge of democracy. Somehow, she cannot plug into the infectious spirit of optimism and victory that is sweeping the country. She appears stricken by a malaise that affects every aspect of her life.

Her work is suffering and her boss is unhappy with her. More importantly, her teenage daughter, Mangi (Mpumi Malatsi), who is deaf, feels neglected and unwanted by her mother. Thandeka wants desperately to form a meaningful relationship with Mangi, who has spent much of her time with her grandparents, but seems completely incapable. It is not through lack of will, but through lack of means; she simply cannot connect with her daughter.

Mangi, a loving child, painstakingly creates for her mother the *Zulu Love Letter* of the film's title. She gives Thandeka chance after chance, but invariably ends up disappointed.

There can be no single reason for Thandeka's coldness, her alienation, but it is certainly linked to her experience of the struggle. She has seen things that she would rather not have seen; things that haunt her every moment. We learn too that Mangi's deafness is linked directly to Thandeka's work and political activities.

Where Thandeka would like nothing more than to look to the future, she is forced to deal with a particularly horrific incident from her past.

Years ago she witnessed a brutal, cold-blooded murder of Dineo, an activist, and now she is confronted by the activist's mother, Me'Tau (Sophie Mgcina), who wants nothing more than to find her daughter's remains and give her a proper burial. Me'Tau needs Thandeka's help.

These two mothers are both, in different ways, searching for their daughters. Me'Tau's unenviable situation perhaps putting Thandeka's strained relationship with her own daughter into perspective.

The apartheid police who killed Dineo and are still operating with impunity, have a lot to lose should Dineo's remains be recovered, and set about intimidating Thandeka and Me'Tau. The consequences are tragic and the film's, somewhat rushed, ending does not impose a neat and happy resolution to a film that is unsuited to a neat and happy resolution.

I like *Zulu Love Letter* very much because it is honest, and because it is angry, and because it takes all sorts of chances and bets on its audience faithfully embarking on the journey.

I am filled with admiration, wonder and relief whenever I see a film that is obviously the result of a director's unique vision, and not just a hotch potch of formulas and focus group interventions. *Zulu Love Letter* is just such a film.

Director's Statement

Ramadan Suleman

△ The Director and cast on set

PRODUCTION

Zulu Love Letter was scheduled to be shot over nine weeks and the date for principal photography was set as 14 April 2003, but we soon experienced problems with the financing of the film. While most of our partners confirmed their participation, one key partner had still to commit to the project. This partner's evaluation process was, frustratingly, much slower than we had anticipated and the delay compromised the start of principal photography and caused problems with the timing because, at the other end, some of the secured funding had to be used before it expired. The result was that the shooting period was cut to six weeks and the implications of the revised schedule had to be factored in for all the elements involved – from script to production.

CASTING

The casting process began long before the shooting script was finalised. Bheki, co-producer Jacques Bidou and I discussed a number of local, continental and international actors to play Thandeka. The challenge was where to find female characters who would represent the long list of strong South African women who have traversed our political and cultural landscape. A South African casting director insisted that we try Pamela Nomvete, who we originally thought was too young for the part. Nomvete was outstanding and showed incredible commitment during her auditions and, subsequently, throughout the production. She was the true incarnation of Stanislovski's method actor. She was also very humble and supportive of the other actors and formed a critical bond with Mpumi Malatsi, who played Simangaliso.

Working with Mpumi Malatsi

The casting of Mangi was definitely the most challenging, both for me personally and for the rest of my key creative team. Simply put, none of us was prepared for the deaf world. We had visited almost all the deaf schools in the Johannesburg area – Kathlehong, Lenasia, Soweto and Rosebank. Then the casting director contacted the Transoranje School for the Deaf in Pretoria. After a number of consultations the school prepared the learners for their auditions, which consisted of a monologue and a relationship exercise. Leigh-Anne Wolmarans, our sign language consultant, was my assistant during this segment of the auditions. I was amazed at how relaxed all the learners seemed in front of the camera but Mpumi stood out because of her strong presence and performance.

We soon discovered the intricacies of the deaf world and also the ignorance and arrogance of the 'speaking world'. For instance, we were oblivious to the various sign language systems within the country and it was only during the first two days of auditions that we were alerted by Leigh-Ann that Mpumi understood only *Afrikaans* sign language. To accommodate Mpumi, Pamela, Connie Mfuku (MaKhumalo), Patrick Ndlovu (Bab'Khumalo) and Kurt Egelhof (Moola) learned basic sign language to try to bridge the communication gap, while, in performance, Pamela had to revert to her own improvised version.

Occasionally during rehearsals I would give instructions with my back turned to Mpumi and Leigh-Ann, completely forgetting that I needed to face them if they were to lip-read my directions. Leigh-Ann would calmly but sternly walk in front of me and remind me to 'look at me when you are talking'. The three weeks of rehearsals eventually helped to create a family with a respectful working method.

Working with the Khulumani Support Group

During the writing process we viewed several documentaries, among them interviews with individuals and members of the Khulumani Support Group – an organisation that represents the victims and survivors of the violent crimes committed by the apartheid state.

The script owes some of its inspiration to personal friends and to artists who were either killed or left traumatised and even mentally ill by their experiences of apartheid violence. The Khulumani Support Group was a powerful extension and embodiment of the need to 'speak out', as their name calls for. As an advocacy group campaigning on behalf of victims and survivors, the achievements or failures of Khulumani remain *the* litmus test of our collective societal seriousness in addressing the horrors of apartheid.

Khulumani's willingness to go into partnership with us and have its members appear as actors in the film was, for us, a singular honour and an inspiring manifestation of their will and struggle not only for truth but also for justice. They were absolutely clear, and insisted, that their appearance in the film was part of their struggle to have their stories told and recorded on film for their great-grandchildren. A series of screenings was organised nationally for Khulumani members and, despite our veteran status in negotiating the responses of local and international audiences, we were relieved, humbled and tremendously touched by their embrace of the completed version of the film.

VISION AND STYLE

One cannot speak of a specific style apart from the inspiration gleaned over the years from several creative sources. We did watch a number of documentaries on the Truth and Reconciliation Commission and, I suppose, ultimately I had the sense that we would need to walk a fine line between reality and fiction, documentary and fantasy. This was particularly the case in relation to how we would shoot the interludes and the 'dream sequences' relating to Thandeka and Mangi. The way they were written translated into an expensive shooting and post-production process that the budget did not allow for.

The challenge became how we could ensure that the interludes were shot and constructed so that viewers would be able to distinguish them from the 'realism' of the main narrative. Yet the interludes had to allow for the entrée into a very different sense of representation; one that disrupts the normal flow of time, realism and interpretation. The aim in the interludes was to suspend disbelief and enter another realm of time, experience and knowledge, which, although bordering on the magical, was still concerned with rethinking what we thought we knew, or saw, or the relationship between fiction and fact. The interludes were also intended to allow us to imagine other possibilities and futures, which, despite their imaginary status, are often much closer to our fears, hopes and dreams.

Manu Teran, the cinematographer, had just returned from a shoot in Kenya where he had experimented with the use of 16 frames per second as a technique to slow down the image. He suggested that the 16-frame-per-second technique might be effective, especially since, when it is used with actors or objects in movement, it is noticeable, but when the actors are motionless it is hardly discernable. Its dynamism lies in the blur – or visual destabilisation it creates – in how one sees and understands movement. The purpose of the technique was to create a subtle transition from the present to the past, without disrupting or isolating the present. In other words, the present is no different from the past.

Since the 16-frames-per-second images were shot without sound we had to go through a two-month sound process with Jean Mallet in Paris, recreating sound effects that would enhance the psychological violence experienced by Thandeka and the other characters. The principle on which Mallet – who has worked on several blockbuster movies – insisted was to guard against using or rendering sound effects that are foreign to the overall feel and realism of the film. In line with his thinking Mallet felt the sound in both the film and the interludes had to be organic; that the film had a tremendous amount of natural sound and we should try as far as possible to use that creatively before resorting to film music or other forms of sound. He was perceptive in this regard and did a great job.

THE TRUTH AND RECONCILIATION COMMISSION

When former President Nelson Mandela's government inaugurated the Truth and Reconciliation Commission (TRC) many in South Africa, across the racial divides, were not pleased, for different reasons. The process involved people registering to testify and their claims being investigated. The final part would then be the testimony in front of the commission. The commission was fraught with problems. Despite the large numbers of people who finally testified they represented only a small percentage of those who had been abused.

Perpetrators qualified for indemnity as long as they made what was called 'full disclosure'. Unfortunately, the majority of victims who testified forgave perpetrators who were neither keen nor willing, to this day, to ask for forgiveness. Furthermore, some former security police agents are now employees of the new government's police, military and intelligence services while others have become private citizens or 'respectable' businessmen and live among the people.

The perpetrators and victims of the apartheid era are now living together in townships and suburbs, but their neighbourliness is often ruptured by the 'return of the past', which ignites suspicion, vengeance, and calls for justice and reparation. However, today, despite our reservations about the TRC, we can proudly say that whatever the outcome, it was done. What the TRC represented was the beginning of a healing process, however limited. The outcome for me is that never again will South Africans be able to say that 'we did not know'.

Zulu Love Letter was filmed nearly a decade after the inauguration of the TRC and still, today, the past continues to haunt South Africa's post-apartheid era. Many of the vestiges of apartheid have been dismantled, especially in the areas of democracy and governance, but when it comes to the economy and social life apartheid is still very much alive. In many ways, the traumas of the past are relived in the continuing racism, violence and extreme disparities that still characterise the country. Mothers are still mourning, families are still

searching for the remains of loved ones, and communities are still divided within themselves and across racial and class lines.

In all post-war, post-conflict and post-dictatorship societies people are challenged to confront and explore psychological traumas emanating from the repression and violence of the past. In many cases, profound emotional dramas played themselves out in families whose way of life was touched and, often, deeply and brutally affected by societal developments. Post-war European countries have taken decades to rebuild shattered familial and communal structures and currently, in some areas, there is a resurgence of violence under the guise of ethnic cleansing. In my opinion, these developments should remind us that we ignore oppression, inequality and the abuse of human rights at our peril. Sooner rather than later the complex issues that we hide, or are unwilling to resolve with honesty and integrity because of our human frailties and fears, will return in more violent and threatening ways. The most we can do is to deal with them in the best way we can, without adopting either the ostrich position or hiding behind a wide range of 'ifs' and 'buts'. The future demands such a commitment from all of us.

△ Khulumani members at TRC registration

No longer at ease

Years after the Truth and Reconciliation Commission, South African film is grappling with its troubled legacy. **Jyoti Mistry** argues that *Zulu Love Letter* may be the most important take on this topic yet

The quest for truth forms the basis of the human condition. Truth is considered desirable, it is what marks humans as creatures with a conscience (a more evolved species from others) and if truth is found, it is considered absolute.

The idea of truth is not contested, because it functions as a higher form of knowledge that cannot be tampered with. In its purest sense truth is often used as an instrument to shape ideas, wield decisions and forge alliances. It is the abstraction (knowledge) through which power is gained and disseminated.

Truth, for many South Africans, carries the burden of the Truth and Reconciliation Commission (TRC) and its vast performative function. Vast because it served to reconcile histories, to build the nation and was a public exhibition that convinced individuals that reconciliation is a political and historical necessity to forge a (national) collective.

It is little wonder then that themes of reconciliation are a preoccupation of recently produced South Africans films. "TRC films" – the likes of *Forgiveness, In My Country* and *Red Dust* – have emerged as a genre capturing a range of films concerned with the experiences of historical trauma, truth-finding/telling and acts of reconciliation and restitution.

Zulu Love Letter, which opened on Friday, pushes the boundaries of this genre. What makes it a significant film is that it contests the notion of truth and reveals that the quest for truth is not as desirable as we may believe and that its outcomes are not necessarily ones for which society may have steeled itself.

Truth comes with the responsibilities of justice. It demands a response from society, to honour the act of disclosing the truth. It is this profound, challenging and uncomfortable alliance between truth and the desire for justice that makes *Zulu Love Letter* compelling.

The story revolves around an activist-turned-investigative-journalist who is seeking the perpetrators of a political assassination she witnessed during the apartheid era. Thandeka Khumalo, portrayed with intensity by Pamela Nomvete, is a character who dedicated her life to the struggle for truth, a struggle that sought to honour a life with dignity. She distrusts the public performance of the TRC. She does not believe that it will offer justice nor return to her the deeply wounded sense of self and loss of dignity she experienced in solitary confinement and under torture.

Throughout the film she remains haunted by the past; the ghosts that bombard her unconscious offer no soothing words of reconciliation and validation of sacrifice for a higher cause. Instead, her body and spirit suffer, says in one scene.

The truth she knows is not manicured and crafted with a political agenda, it is visceral – and it demands justice, not just for herself, but for the collective who are euphoric from the performance of the TRC. This desire for justice and personal reconciliation develops through the story of another woman Me'Tau (Sophie Mgcina) seeking a dignified burial for her daughter. These two women are bound by the trauma of their experiences and the desire for an act of justice that responds to the disclosure of truths.

As in their earlier film *Fools*, writer and director team Bheki Peterson and Ramadan Suleman have set themselves a challenging task – of dealing with the psyche of women taunted and scarred by a social and political system that neither protects nor understands them. The women in *Zulu Love Letter* cannot trust institutional frameworks to voice their trauma. Instead, they have to find alternatives to seek justice. Me'Tau steals a visit to Thandeka to ask for assistance in locating her daughter's remains rather than going to the police.

Film theorist Susan Hayward, in her analysis of cinema and nation formation, observes that the female body in film is used as an allegory for the birthing and building of a (new) nation. Thandeka's story is as allegorical as it is personal. She has been physically and psychologically violated so that a new nation might be forged through possession of her body. In her personal life she attempts to reconcile with her deaf daughter Mangi (Mpumi Malatsi) with whom she has a strained relationship. That she has not learned sign language in order to communicate with her daughter, is symbolic.

> The world seems to be full of those who `serve truth', yet the virtue of justice is rarely present . . . The truth is that few serve truth because few possess the pure will to justice' – Friedrich Nietzsche

Most representations of activists' lives reinforce the myth that the political struggle was at no cost to the personal and that any price paid was for a greater good. *Zulu Love Letter* takes on this taboo, revealing the devastating effects wrought on interpersonal relationships by apartheid and the struggle.

Thandeka wants to be a good mother and to offer Mangi the kind of support she needs. But by participating in the struggle, interpersonal relationships have become dysfunctional.

In a powerful reversal of roles, the daughter offers her mother astute observations about her interpersonal relationships, reflecting the troubled socialising processes that a history of violence has created in a generation of activists. The liberation struggle subsumed the possibilities for complex identity formation and instead privileged a political agenda.

What will disturb South African audiences most is that the truth here is not the homogenised and generously reconciled version of the past that we have found in TRC films to date. *Zulu Love Letter* takes on the dangerous challenge of showing up the anger, the fractured and damaged psyche that our history has dealt us. It challenges South Africans to examine that anger; the alienation and the uneasy feeling that justice might not have been fully served.

The TRC systemically repressed experiences of trauma so that all South Africans might participate in a new social order. But as Sigmund Freud warned, the repressed returns in the form of the uncanny and challenges the order that has been so consciously created.

Zulu Love Letter will leave audiences with a feeling of unease, because our history and our trauma is one of unease. The film sets a new precedent in TRC films. Here is an evolution in the genre that reveals the truth from the position of the personal and the subjective. It does not rationalise violence nor does it glorify nation formation as wilful acts of personal sacrifice and martyrdom.

Thandeka's suffering exposes the depth and price of personal suffering to gain human equity and dignity. But that suffering demands recognition through justice. This film reveals the tensions between the desire for truth, the need for forgiveness and the all-consuming necessity for justice.

Silence speaks powerfully of hidden pain

BY **MOJE MOKONE**

Victor Hugo's statement that "music expresses that which cannot be put in words but which may not remain silent" came into my mind while watching *Zulu Love Letter*.

It confronts the questions of residual anger, guilt and stress that borders on mental disorder. All threaten to break the bonds between mothers and daughters, families and communities.

Grief and trauma are frustratingly difficult to describe, but the film succeeds in capturing them through the thoughtful depiction of the relationship between three generations of women.

There is the complex lead character, Thandeka (powerfully portrayed by Pamela Nomvete), her deaf daughter, Mangi (Mpami Malatsi, who commands a colossal presence at odds with her muteness), and Me'Tau (Sophie Mgcina). Whether the women choose not to "remain silent" or try to cope by deliberately forgetting, the trauma lingers on like a song that insists on being rehearsed to death.

The film starts at a moment of crisis and unfolds at a subtle pace, tensely poised between the breakdown and healing of Thandeka. The story has no simple linear structure – perhaps to underscore the overwhelming confusion of the post-apartheid era.

Thandeka's consciousness is conveyed in sombre cinematography with minimalist tones, pared dialogue and dark, gloomy interiors that contrast with the sunny barrenness of the township landscape.

There is little background music. Its haunting absence draws you into the silence and the moody, natural sounds that mark the ebb and flow of Thandeka's mind. Only towards the end does Me'Tau's contralto lend poignancy to the funereal dirges that were so much part of the burials during the 1970s and '80s.

Thandeka, an ex-activist and journalist, is in a democratic South Africa still stuck in a mental state where past and present coexist. Her limbo stems from the difficult relationship she has with Mangi because of her previous role, which led to her being an absent mother during the struggle.

Then there is her self-conscious preoccupation with the political past: her detention and torture, the murders at the behest of the apartheid state of her friend and colleague, photographer Michael Peters (Richard Nzimande), and student activist Dineo Tau, who was assassinated while Thandeka and Peters looked on helplessly.

The horror of the crimes – in which her guilt is misplaced and she believes she colluded with the police – disturbs her deeply. Anxiety leads to panic attacks and writer's block, and makes her afraid of committing herself to relationships. One moment she is streetwise, gentle, beautiful and seductive, and the next she becomes a snarling face, spitting expletives through a twisted mouth.

The appearance of ghosts from the past – in the form of Me'Tau, the mother of Dineo, and Dhlamini (Samson Khumalo), an accomplice in the assassination of Dineo – propels Thandeka into action.

She summons her journalistic and investigative skills to help Me'Tau to find the remains of Dineo and other victims for proper burial. She becomes the thread weaving through a necklace of beads – the Zulu love letter – started by Mangi as a gift to her mother.

The *Zulu Love Letter*, as an artistic expression, is dazzling in its creativity, profound in the way it looks at the past and the future simultaneously, and eloquent in the way in which it shows that words are often overrated and other forms of expression underrated.

Mangi's love letter takes its inspiration from tradition and beads, but incorporates all that is contemporary, including bottle caps. She identifies with dilemma, contradiction and confusion, vicariously taking part in the tragic events of an enigmatic past – a political past that is so difficult to understand or describe in ordinary, everyday speech and language, including sign language.

She epitomises stark surrealism – the strange feeling of being in the music, playing along – being part in all but time and space.

For Mangi, no words are ever sufficient to recapture the magic of the music of the secret place, "the hiding place", evocatively captured here in dream-like sequences.

One ought not to read simplistic, didactic messages into *Zulu Love Letter*. The film seeks to cajole, chaperone and coerce reflection on the real, daily trials and tribulations of ordinary people, the ones who do not speak in meaningless soundbites and are therefore not sexy enough to be heard.

Zulu Love Letter is the stringing together of an eerie narrative of a family, a dead friend, an ex-lover, a venal councillor and incompetent police, all caught up in the unfinished business of their past, desperately trying to excise the trauma of apartheid.

For many people, the jury is still out about the catharsis that the Truth and Reconciliation Commission was meant to deliver.

AWARDS

SCRIPT

Special Jury Prize – Best Script 2001, France, 15th Edition, Grand Prix du Meilleur Scenariste, 29 October 2001, Paris.

FILM

- Tanit D'Argent (Silver) – Carthage International Film Festival, 2004 (Tunisia)
- Grand Prize – Festival International du Film d'Amour, 2005 (Mons, Belgium)
- European Union Award – Fespaco, 2005 (Burkina Faso)
- Best Actress – Pamela Nomvete Marimbe, Fespaco, 2005 (Burkina Faso)
- Unicef Prize for the Promotion of Women's Rights – Fespaco, 2005 (Burkina Faso)
- 9th INALCO Prize (National Institute of Eastern Languages and Civilizations) – Fespaco, 2005 (Burkina Faso)
- Best Actress – Mpumi Malatsi, Capetown World Cinema Festival, 2005
- Special Jury Prize – Durban International Film Festival, 2005 (South Africa)
- Public Award for Feature Film – Cinema d' Afrique, Angiers, France, 2005
- Human Rights Award, The Mar del Plata International Film Festival, 2006 (Argentina)

OFFICIAL SELECTIONS

Zulu Love Letter received more than a dozen official invitations to premier international film festivals including the Venice International Film Festival (Venezia 61 orrizonti), 2004; Toronto International Film Festival, 2004; Fespaco (Burkina Faso), 2005; and the American Film Institute Los Angeles Festival, 2005.

FILM CREDITS

KEY CAST

Thandeka	Pamela Nomvete Marimbe
Simangaliso	Mpumi Malatsi
Me'Tau	Sophie Mgcina
Moola	Kurt Egelhof
Bouda'D	Hugh Masebenza
MaKhumalo	Connie Mfuku

KEY CREW

Director	Ramadan Suleman
Screenplay	Bhekizizwe Peterson & Ramadan Suleman
Cinematographer	Manuel Teran
Editor	Jacques Comets
Sound Editor	Jean Mallet
Sound Mix	Jean-Pierre Laforce
Music	Original South African music
Art Direction	Patrick Dechesne & Alain-Pascal Housiaux
Producers	Jacques Bidou, Bhekizizwe Peterson, Marianne Dumoulin, Ramadan Suleman

PRODUCTION COMPANIES

SOUTH AFRICA	Natives At Large Bhekizizwe Peterson & Ramadan Suleman
FRANCE	JBA Production Jacques Bidou & Marianne Dumoulin
A co-production	Hollybell (South Africa) Natives At Large (South Africa) JBA Production (France) FMB2 Films (France) ZDF Arte & ZDF/Das kleine Fernsehspiel (Germany)
in association with	IDC (South Africa) & NFVF (South Africa)
with support from	Fonds Sud Cinéma (Ministère des Affaires Etrangères & CNC – France) European Commission (Fonds Européen de Développement)
and	SABC (South Africa) Yle tv1 co-production (Finland) Church Development Service EED (Germany)

The script was supported by the 5th Script Development Fund Ciné-Sud-Amiens International Film Festival – 2000

△ Bhekizizwe Peterson and Ramadan Suleman on the set of *Fools*.

Picture by Cedric Nunn

a screenplay

by BHEKIZIZWE PETERSON AND RAMADAN SULEMAN

ZULU LOVE LETTER

1 INT: HILLBROW – THANDEKA'S BLOCK OF FLATS – UNDERGROUND PARKING GARAGE – NIGHT

The garage is filled with cars. A resolute 60-year-old black security guard, **NTATE NO-NONSENSE**, in uniform and carrying a baton, is talking into his walkie-talkie. His words are inaudible because of the noise of a free-jazz track coming from a **VW POLO** parked in one of the parking bays, behind a pillar. The door on the driver's side of the **POLO** is wide open and the driver's head, slouched on the steering wheel, rests against the hooter. The driver is **THANDEKA KHUMALO**, a 38-year-old journalist on the weekly newspaper, the Mail & Guardian.

NO-NONSENSE lifts **THANDEKA's** head from the steering wheel and lets it rest against the headrest. He then moves to the passenger side of the car and removes the CD from the player. The music stops. He returns his attention to **THANDEKA**, who is dressed formally and has her journalist identity card pinned to her jacket. Next to her feet is a pool of vomit.

2 INT: HILLBROW – THANDEKA'S BLOCK OF FLATS – UNDERGROUND PARKING GARAGE – NIGHT

THANDEKA is lying on a stretcher that is being loaded hastily into an ambulance. An oxygen mask covers her nose and mouth. **NO-NONSENSE** and a few onlookers observe the scene. The ambulance departs.

3 INT: AMBULANCE - STREET - NIGHT

THANDEKA is lying immobile on the stretcher surrounded by electronic monitoring equipment as the ambulance speeds through the streets of Johannesburg. She is still wearing the oxygen mask and two drips are suspended over her head, their tubes feeding into veins in her left arm. The sound of the siren and the monitor's monotonous beep echo in the ambulance.

INTERLUDE A

A 1

In **THANDEKA's** mind's eye she enters a blurred, greyish landscape.

A 2

A black **TOYOTA COROLLA** drives slowly through the changing landscape. The **COROLLA** is simultaneously spy and sniper. A long-range camera lens protrudes, like a pistol, through the passenger window.

A 3

The point of view of the vignettes is similar to that of an eye focusing through the viewfinder of a camera. It registers three different posters carrying banner headlines highlighting the social, economic and political state of the nation: 'National State of Emergency Declared'; 'Countrywide Swoop on Black Journalists'; 'Pre-Election Violence Predicted'.

A 4

A voice is heard addressing a rally.

MAN

[off]

The people of South Africa ... freedom ... want peace. This is our message to the government.

4 INT: JOHANNESBURG HOSPITAL - MORNING

A drip stand begins to form and takes over the screen. The tube of the drip leads downwards until it reaches past the tranquil face of **THANDEKA**, who is in a bed in the Johannesburg Hospital. **THANDEKA's** frail hands are tenderly massaging the left shoulder of her fourteen-year-old daughter, **SIMANGALISO**, who is sitting half turned away from her mother. **SIMANGALISO's** piercing stare is steadfastly focused on a bouquet of orange flowers on a small side table next to the bed.

INTERLUDE B

B 1 SFX

SIMANGALISO is imagining that her gaze makes the flowers wilt, one by one, down the sides of the vase.

4a INT: JOHANNESBURG HOSPITAL - MORNING

Noticing her daughter's distracted look **THANDEKA** squeezes the girl's shoulder blades firmly, returning her attention to the room. **SIMANGALISO** returns to the present looking uneasy and takes a final look at the flowers, which are still upright.

Still looking at **SIMANGALISO**, **THANDEKA** picks up a birthday party invitation that is lying on the bed.

THANDEKA

[mouthing and signing]

You and your father can start to send out these invitations. I'll be out of here long before your birthday. And if not, this ward is big enough for one hell of a party.

SIMANGALISO looks at her mother with indifference.

INTERLUDE C

C 1

The screen goes black and white and snowy as the black **TOYOTA COROLLA** screeches around a township street corner in slow motion. It is pursuing two isolated figures – a young man and a young girl. The **COROLLA** stops briefly and we see the boots of one person emerging from the car before it takes off again. The person is **MICHAEL GREEN**, a white man in his mid-thirties; well built and with rugged blond hair. Only his back is visible. **GREEN** is hip looking and carries himself confidently, a demeanour which, coupled with his looks, gives him the air of someone who has just stepped out of a Camel cigarette advertisement. He is wearing a long brown coat on top of his informal attire. He calmly follows the girl.

C 2

THANDEKA and **MICHAEL PETERS**, who are in a nearby church, run to a window.

C 3

The youths separate at an intersection, the girl running into the yard outside the church. She is **DINEO TAU**, a striking looking twenty-year-old. Fear and anguish are initially written all over her face but are

quickly replaced by a look of calm resignation, a deep acceptance of death. She looks back at the **COROLLA.**

The **COROLLA** comes to a halt less than two metres away from **DINEO**, who, with the wall of a house behind her, is cornered. She stops and assesses her situation, breathing heavily, like a tired buffalo after a stampede. **GREEN** pulls out a revolver and walks purposefully towards the girl.

C 4

THANDEKA, in jeans and a T-shirt, is huddled adjacent to a window next to a pew. She is clutching a notepad and next to her **MICHAEL PETERS**, a photographer, is taking pictures of **DINEO's** ordeal as if his life depends on it.

DINEO, in a last attempt to proclaim her personhood, raises a defiant clenched fist proclaiming black power, her lips clearly screaming an inaudible 'Amandla Awethu [Power is Ours]!'.

4b INT: JOHANNESBURG HOSPITAL - MORNING

THANDEKA is brooding over her recollection of **DINEO's** assassination.

DINEO

[off]

Amandla Awethu! Power to the people!

C 5

Without much thought or any fanfare **GREEN** simply stops a metre from the girl. He is joined by two more assassins. One is **SIBUSISO DHLAMINI**, a fortysomething black man of average height and weight, dressed in a suit. Next to him is **BERTHUS MOOLMAN**, an Afrikaner in his forties, clad in a grey suit. Both wear long brown coats identical to that worn by **GREEN**.

The three men stand in front of **DINEO** and **GREEN** raises his gun without any thought and cocks it. A shot cuts the stillness and echoes through the landscape.

C 6

THANDEKA, overcome by her emotions and the teargas, hunches her body into a foetal position, trembling and shaking all over. **PETERS** finally holds her, burying his head in her shaking shoulders.

5 INT: CITY - MAIL & GUARDIAN NEWSROOM - LATE MORNING

THANDEKA walks into the offices of the Mail & Guardian, greeting and smiling at a few colleagues as she makes her way to her desk. At the sight of **THANDEKA**, **LAURICE KATZ** comes running towards her. **KATZ** is in her mid-thirties, dressed casually but oozing style and class. The two embrace and hug each other like long-lost friends.

KATZ

Chom!

THANDEKA

Chom.

KATZ

You had me shit scared, chom. Shit. What happened?

THANDEKA

I just had a blackout.

KATZ

Blackout? They told me you were in a coma.

They arrive at **THANDEKA's** desk where **THABISO**, a young black man in his early twenties, wearing a finely cut suit and tie, is sitting.

THANDEKA

No. No coma. So, what's going on?

KATZ

I forgot to tell you, the frog has been ringing the changes left, right and centre.

THANDEKA

O, Jesus!

KATZ

Thandeka, are you okay?

THANDEKA

Ja, I'm fine. Really.

KATZ notices **DICK SMITH**, a white man in his mid-fifties, the image of a proverbial editor, who has been watching **THANDEKA'S** noisy arrival.

KATZ

The frog, quack, quack.

KATZ leaves as **THANDEKA** notices **SMITH** beckoning to her to come to his office.

THANDEKA approaches **THABISO**, who is working at the computer, apparently oblivious to her.

THANDEKA

I'm back now, okay. Thanks for looking after my desk. Now get lost. Hey, bye-bye.

THABISO collects his jacket and departs without saying a word.

6 INT: CITY - MAIL & GUARDIAN - SMITH'S OFFICE - LATE MORNING

THANDEKA is sitting in **SMITH**'s office. He is standing in front of his desk looking at her sternly. The walls of the office are covered with pictures of 'relevant' leaders and headlines, and certificates reflecting several media awards. Occupying pride of place is a framed, enlarged newspaper cutting of the picture **PETERS** took of **DINEO** giving her defiant black-power salute.

THANDEKA

[in a measured tone]

Look, I don't know what's going on ... I've told you ... I just can't write. I'm constantly tired. My head is full of things I want to say but I just cannot string a sentence together ...

SMITH

Your head has always been full of things but it never seemed to affect your performance in the past!

THANDEKA snaps in response to this remark.

THANDEKA

Oh ... you son of a bitch! First it was Michael Peters, now it's me? You suck us dry and then just spit us out!

SMITH

Spare me the sermon, my girl. Peters was a nervous wreck, incapable of taking useable pictures to save his miserable life!

THANDEKA

You bastard! If you had not delivered him to the security police ...

SMITH

I never did such a thing!

THANDEKA

You sold us out!

SMITH

That's the truth!

THANDEKA

All your liberal values and defence of human rights disappeared when it came to the crunch ... It was nice and fine when we brought you the scoops, but when it came to putting your fat-white-liberal-arse on the line ... the best you could do was hide behind all sorts of legalities!

SMITH

How many times must I tell you that your files were subpoenaed! You are not the only journalist on this newspaper that's lived through a state of emergency so please, please, spare me your tantrums! Now ... the long and the short of it is that your account, your entertainment allowance is cancelled, you can hand in your petrol card to dispatch at the end of the day.

THANDEKA continues to stare in front of her. SMITH realises she is not going to respond.

SMITH

You can use your desk until further notice.

THANDEKA

Thank you, your majestic piece of white liberal-arsed scum ... I should have seen it coming. You can pick and choose your black staff now ... [*She points out of the window.*] Look at the crop of affirmative action snot-noses that you have at your disposal ... nose-brigade cases who think that being black is a job description and that 'the struggle' refers to which cellular network they should subscribe to. Well, fuck you all.

7 INT: NORTHERN SUBURBS - ST MARY'S SCHOOL - CLASSROOM - DAY

SIMANGALISO is standing at the head of a circle of **GIRLS**, all in school uniform. Spread out in front of **SIMANGALISO** is her bead project. **A TEACHER** is sitting on a chair just outside the circle.

SIMANGALISO

[signing very deliberately to her audience]

Why did his parents abandon him? Why?

8 EXT: NORTHERN SUBURBS - ST MARY'S SCHOOL - CORRIDOR - DAY

THANDEKA is walking down the corridor.

9 INT: NORTHERN SUBURBS - ST MARY'S SCHOOL - PRINCIPAL'S OFFICE - DAY

PRINCIPAL SMUTS, a dour looking white nun in her late fifties, is sitting behind her imposing desk. The office is modestly decorated with religious artefacts.

SMUTS

Simangaliso's performance in the exams was not as good as we have come to expect of her. Sloppy in places, but then that is usual at their age ... so many things start to vie for their attention. She's also, of course, anxious about leaving the school. We are going to miss her.

[silence]

SMUTS gets up and starts to display a series of beautiful, colourful paintings that have been carefully placed on the top right-hand corner of her desk. Each of the paintings is signed **'MANGI'**. **SMUTS** stands next to **THANDEKA**.

THANDEKA

These are beautiful. Can I have them?

SMUTS

Of course ... *[She draws some of the paintings together and spreads them out in front of THANDEKA.]* There is something that her drama and arts teachers have drawn my attention to ... Lately, her work is full of anguish and, while it is still very good, it is disconcerting for a child to be dealing with the issues we are noticing in her work. Are there problems at home that we should know about, Ms Khumalo?

Silence as both women take a second to study the drawings more closely.

10 EXT: NORTHERN SUBURBS - ST MARY'S SCHOOL - YARD - DAY

THANDEKA and **SMUTS** are ambling down a pathway running through the school's flourishing garden.

SMUTS

Here in this environment all the girls are 'normal'... to use a word I absolutely detest. Here they have many ways of speaking and hearing, whether it's by sign language, art, lip reading, feeling vibrations. In fact, here, it is you who are disabled. *[silence]* Can you sign, Ms Khumalo?

SMUTS hesitates after her question. **THANDEKA** does not answer and simply walks on. The nun resumes her walk and catches up with **THANDEKA.** The two walk on, intimidated by the silence that has imposed itself between them.

11 EXT: GOLDEN HIGHWAY - AFTERNOON

THANDEKA is driving on the Golden Highway, moving away from the city. **SIMANGALISO** is sitting next to her, still in her school uniform. The two, although aware of each other's presence, are wrapped up in their own thoughts.

12 EXT: SOWETO - TOWNSHIP STREET - AFTERNOON

THANDEKA steers the car carefully in and out of a water-filled ditch on a sandy township road while stealing glances at the township life around her. The **POLO** finally pulls up next to a small, neat house with a striking green garden that looks like an oasis in the barren surroundings.

THANDEKA and **SIMANGALISO** alight. **SIMANGALISO** disappears into the house. **THANDEKA's** attention is caught by someone calling out to her. She walks towards the sound and encounters **BOUDA'D**, a man in his mid-twenties. Two women dressed in mourning walk past. **BOUDA'D** is rugged and carries a homemade wire cage with two pigeons crammed inside.

BOUDA'D

T-man, T-man, hola, hola, hola. Wat se 'mshana [What's up friend]?

THANDEKA

Hola! Bouda'D ...

BOUDA'D

Bouda means brother and D is for dangerous. Is the brotherhood in danger? Or is the brother dangerous? I don't know! Ah T-man, ungangilahli [don't forsake me].

THANDEKA walks away.

BOUDA'D

Don't desert me.

13 INT: SOWETO - KHUMALO RESIDENCE - LOUNGE - AFTERNOON

BAB'KHUMALO and **MAKHUMALO** are seated in the lounge. The old man is noisily sipping tea. A copy of the Mail & Guardian is lying long-forgotten on the couch.

MAKHUMALO has a woven African bowl on her lap, full of multi-coloured beads, each colour in its own transparent plastic bag. There is a quick knock on the door and before anyone can start the ritual of greeting **THANDEKA** enters.

THANDEKA

Sanibonani Baba. Hello Ma.

MAKHUMALO

Hello Thandi.

The others return her greeting. **THANDEKA** places her bag on the dining-room table and returns.

THANDEKA

Eish, I don't smell any supper? Niyazi yini I am hungry ... You know what, I am hungry.

This elicits a sharp look from **BAB'KHUMALO**.

SIMANGALISO comes into the room having changed into casual clothes. She is carrying a rucksack with the bead project tucked into the back pocket.

THANDEKA

[noticing the rucksack]

Mangi, you going to spend the weekend with your father again? What about me?

BAB'KHUMALO

Yes. What about you? Uyakhumbula ngitheni kuwe my girl? Ngithe qaphela ... one day when you want to come back, hopefully there'll be somebody waiting for you. Do you remember what I said to you my girl? I said, be careful ...

Realising that she has opened herself up for attack **THANDEKA** decides to drop the subject.

SIMANGALISO sits next to her grandmother. **MAKHUMALO** opens the rucksack and puts the beads inside the bag. **SIMANGALISO** looks at the different colours, steals a glance at her grandmother and they exchange smiles. They converse using sign language punctuated with verbal interjections and translations from **MAKHUMALO**.

MAKHUMALO

Colours? How you use them it's a trick remember? Blue is ...?

SIMANGALISO

Hope and warmth ... red is the fire of love ...

MAKHUMALO

It also suggests ... a longing ... a heart bleeding for love ...

SIMANGALISO

As well ... blue ... same ... some other days ... blue warm, some days it makes you feel away from things ...

MAKHUMALO

Yes, it depends on how you surround your blues ... with white - for purity and love ... pink is a barren colour ... black is a suggestion of grief ...

THANDEKA

Ma, I'm sorry, but if there's one thing the Black Consciousness Movement is supposed to have taught us ... it is that black is beautiful and white is far from being pure and innocent.

MAKHUMALO is visibly upset by the comment but is at a loss for words. Angry, the old woman disappears into her bedroom. **SIMANGALISO** directs a long and discourteous stare at her mother, who looks back at her nonchalantly.

SIMANGALISO

Why?

SIMANGALISO takes her rucksack and dashes into the bedroom.

14 INT: SOWETO - KHUMALO RESIDENCE - BEDROOM - AFTERNOON

SIMANGALISO walks into her grandparents' bedroom and finds **MAKHUMALO** sitting in front of the mirror. She is clearly in great pain and is massaging her left hand. Noticing **SIMANGALISO, MAKHUMALO** puts on a brave face. **SIMANGALISO** takes in the scene without any movement or words and then slowly takes her grandmother's left hand into both of hers, trying to heal it with her warmth. **MAKHUMALO** gives **SIMANGALISO** a smile and a look of reassurance, gently massaging the young girl's hair with her free right hand.

MAKHUMALO

[signing]

Excuse me. I am behaving like a silly old woman. Wait.

SIMANGALISO

[signing]

No, no, no.

MAKHUMALO opens a wooden kist that is standing against the wall, removes a neatly folded cloth which she places on her lap and beckons **SIMANGALISO** to sit next to her. Gently unfolding the cloth **MAKHUMALO** reveals a stunning array of hand-made jewellery and beads. Selecting a dazzling necklace from the pile she slowly, deliberately, holds it in front of **SIMANGALISO.**

MAKHUMALO

[signing and verbalising]

We have little say in the ties of the family that bind us, so we may as well just celebrate. This necklace your grandfather gave me when he left for the city. Take it and keep it safely. It will remind you of us.

SIMANGALISO gently runs her fingers through the beads of the necklace.

15 INT: SOWETO - KHUMALO RESIDENCE - LOUNGE - AFTERNOON

THANDEKA and **BAB'KHUMALO** are at each other's throats.

THANDEKA

Why is everyone on my case? Ma is going on as if Moola's departure means the end of the world. If he is leaving, so what? When I first brought him here I don't recall any of you getting excited.

BAB'KHUMALO

Do not use the past against me. I was no less hostile to Moola than to any of your other boyfriends.

THANDEKA

Yebo ... angithi bekulula ukum'zonda [Yes, but he was easier to hate], who ever heard of a good Indian?

BAB'KHUMALO

Inkosi ingixolele [God forgive me], I would be lying if I said I was not horrified to hear that you are having a child with an Indian. But I opened my arms and welcomed him into my heart and my house.

THANDEKA

Manje inkinga yini [So what's the problem]?

BAB'KHUMALO

I don't believe you ...

THANDEKA

You don't believe what, Baba?

BAB'KHUMALO

I suppose ... kuyafana angithi? Ukuthola Kwakho uSimangaliso awuzange ubuze uMa wakho noma mina ukuthi sisafuna yini ukuba abazali futhi [I guess it's the same, isn't it? You had a child without asking us whether we wanted to be parents again]. We brought her up while you were toyi-toying. And now you simply expect us to adjust to not having her around, my dear!

THANDEKA

But who said she was leaving with him?

BAB'KHUMALO is excited by the appearance of a figure about to enter the house. There is a knock on the door.

BAB'KHUMALO

Awu, nangu umfana wami [Ah, here's my boy]. Come in Moola.

At **BAB'KHUMALO'S** response **MOOLA** enters. **SIMANGALISO** returns, walks up to her father and gives him a warm hug.

MOOLA

Awu Bab'Khumalo. Unjani Baba [How are you, Father]?

BAB'KHUMALO

Kuhle ukukubona mfana wami [Nice to see you, son].

MAKHUMALO

How are you, son?

MOOLA

I'm very well Ma. How you doing?

MAKHUMALO

Bengisathi ngicambalala kancane. Kuyashisa akubekezeleleki [I just had a short nap. The heat is unbearable].

SIMANGALISO enters with two glasses of water for her father and grandfather.

MOOLA

Thank you, baby. Listen, fetch your stuff, we will go soon. *[indicating SIMANGALISO]* I still have to take her home and feed her, Papa.

THANDEKA

No, why don't you come to my place and I'll make us something special?

BAB'KHUMALO

The last time ngivule leyafridge, beyingenalutho [I looked in that fridge, it was full of air].

THANDEKA

Things do change, dear father.

BAB'KHUMALO

Ngebhadi-ke, abantu abajiki [Unfortunately, people seldom change].

The old man's caustic response introduces a layer of tension. Everyone waits for someone to break it, but nothing happens.

16 EXT: HILLBROW – THANDEKA'S FLAT – STREET – LATE AFTERNOON

MOOLA'S TOYOTA COROLLA pulls up next to a four-storey block of flats on a busy Hillbrow street. **MOOLA** and **SIMANGALISO** get out of the car and walk towards the entrance of the flats.

MOOLA

[signing]

Your bead project ... did you get your results?

SIMANGALISO

I got a good grade. My bead project will be a gift for Mom.

THANDEKA comes out of the underground garage, carrying her bag and Simangaliso's paintings. Across the road, she sees a **BLACK TOYOTA COROLLA**, nestled amid the hustle of pedestrians. She hands the drawings to **MOOLA**.

THANDEKA

Just hold this for a second.

THANDEKA hesitates momentarily then, with a determined look, makes her way towards the car. She knocks on the window on the driver's side and is confronted by a puzzled young **MAN** moving his head in time to the rap music thundering out of the car's CD player.

THANDEKA

I'm sorry. Sorry.

Smiling, **THANDEKA** turns and makes her way back to **MOOLA** and **SIMANGALISO**. The three walk towards the block of flats.

<u>17 INT: HILLBROW - THANDEKA'S FLAT - KITCHEN - NIGHT</u>

THANDEKA, knife in hand, is in the kitchen preparing supper. After a while she quietly steals a glance at **MOOLA** and **SIMANGALISO** from the kitchen door. The two are noisily at play in the lounge and are oblivious to her presence. **THANDEKA** returns her attention to her cooking.

<u>18 INT: HILLBROW - THANDEKA'S FLAT - DININGROOM/LOUNGE - NIGHT</u>

The walls of the flat are adorned with a carefully selected collection of African art, including photographs, paintings, posters and clay pots. In the one corner we can see that some of **Simangaliso's** paintings occupy pride of place. The lounge is littered with an imposing number of shelves creaking under the weight of books, records and CDs. **MOOLA** and **SIMANGALISO** are involved in a fierce karate contest. The battle is interrupted by the sound of the doorbell. Two side lights in the diningroom and lounge flicker on and off in tandem with the sound. On hearing the bell **MOOLA** heaves himself up and gently tosses **SIMANGALISO** onto her back. **SIMANGALISO** gets up, tidies herself and watches **MOOLA**.

MOOLA opens the door and is confronted by **SIPHO MTHEMBU**, an impressive looking man in his mid-thirties, smartly clad in long pants and a skipper and looking not unlike a professional golfer. He is carrying a bunch of flowers. **MOOLA** steps back and welcomes him in.

THANDEKA

(off)

Ubani [Who is it]?

The two men look at each other, wondering who is supposed to answer.

MOOLA

Hi. My name is Essop Moola.

SIPHO

Sipho Mthembu ... pleased to meet you.

MOOLA

Likewise.

SIPHO

Is Thandeka in?

MOOLA

[in the direction of the kitchen]

It's for you.

THANDEKA comes into the room. On seeing SIPHO consternation spreads over her face.

THANDEKA

Have you met?

SIPHO

Yes.

MOOLA

Ja, we just introduced ourselves.

THANDEKA

Good.

SIPHO

[giving THANDEKA the flowers]

These are for you. Welcome back. I didn't know that you had company ... oh ... I bought tickets for the game. Did you get my message?

THANDEKA

[taking the flowers]

Yes, thanks. I got your message.

[She gives SIPHO a quick kiss.]

The conversation is interrupted by **SIMANGALISO** who is drawing their attention to the fact that the food is burning.

SIMANGALISO

[signing frantically]

Fire ... fire.

MOOLA

I think your food is burning.

THANDEKA

Ah, shit.

MOOLA

Excuse me.

MOOLA and **THANDEKA** rush into the kitchen, leaving **SIMANGALISO** and **SIPHO** staring at each other.

19 INT: HILLBROW - THANDEKA'S FLAT - KITCHEN - NIGHT

THANDEKA grabs the smoking pan, removes it from the stove and dumps it on the balcony floor.

THANDEKA

No, no, no, shit!

She looks at the blackened mess that was her loving gesture to **MOOLA** and **SIMANGALISO** and turns to **MOOLA** with a look of resignation.

20 EXT: HILLBROW - THANDEKA'S FLAT - BALCONY - NIGHT

MOOLA stands at the door of the balcony, looking at **THANDEKA.**

THANDEKA

I'm sorry. I was going to introduce you and Mangi to him under more controlled circumstances.

MOOLA moves to stand next to **THANDEKA.** Unable to bear his disappointed look, **THANDEKA** goes back inside the flat.

21 INT: HILLBROW - THANDEKA'S FLAT - KITCHEN - NIGHT

THANDEKA

Have you been telling people that Mangi will be leaving with you?

MOOLA

No. What people?

THANDEKA

Well, my parents, the school principal ...

MOOLA

I never said a word to anybody. Although I have been making some enquiries about schools in the area.

THANDEKA

Well, I haven't decided whether she is leaving with you or not.

MOOLA

Ja, but it's what she wants. She wants to be with you, she wants to be with her grandparents, but she's not sure of you and what you want.

[silence]

THANDEKA pours herself a glass of water and goes and sits at the table.

MOOLA

Look, I'm going to see a farm in Mpumalanga at the weekend. Would you like to come with us?

THANDEKA

[looking melancholy]

Ja, why not? How I wish I could do what you are doing.

MOOLA

What?

THANDEKA

Just change ... find the hope, the newness.

MOOLA

Look Thandi, you know that you can come and stay with us, any time you like, as long as you like, with no strings attached. You know that.

THANDEKA

Ja, but why do you have to go?

MOOLA

Because there's nothing for me here. I'm just a country boy who came to the city to lure you away and I failed. Now I must go back to the land. But enough about me. How are you doing? Are you sleeping properly? Are you eating better?

THANDEKA

On and off. I've stopped taking the sleeping pills, though. Sometimes, I swear, they kick in during the middle of the day. Familiar faces from the past, familiar things, they all seem to be mocking me.

MOOLA moves to **THANDEKA** and tries to console her by gently massaging her shoulders. **THANDEKA,** uncomfortable with **MOOLA's** gesture, gets up and leaves the room with a deep look of melancholy.

<u>22 INT: HILLBROW - THANDEKA'S FLAT - DININGROOM/LOUNGE - NIGHT</u>

THANDEKA and **MOOLA** are standing in the hallway. **SIMANGALISO** collects her rucksack and leaves without saying goodbye to **THANDEKA. MOOLA** pulls her back and **SIMANGALISO** reluctantly offers her cheek to her mother. **THANDEKA** kisses it gently. **MOOLA** and **SIMANGALISO** go, leaving **THANDEKA** and **SIPHO** looking and feeling awkward.

<u>23 INT: CITY - MAIL & GUARDIAN NEWSPAPER GENERAL OFFICE - MORNING</u>

THANDEKA is absorbedly working at her PC. She does not notice the arrival of an elderly woman in her seventies. **ME'TAU** is dressed as if she is in mourning: all in black, including her doek. **ME'TAU** stands silently for a moment, about a metre away from **THANDEKA,** determined not to disturb her. After a while, **ME'TAU** decides to sit down, her movement suddenly attracting **THANDEKA's** attention.

ME'TAU

Ntshwarelo ngwanaka ... Ne ke sa ikwemisetsa ho o tsosa. Le kae [Forgive me my child ... I did not intend to scare you. How are you]?

THANDEKA

I'm fine Ma, how are you?

ME'TAU

Ke mo ka mohau wa Morena [I am still alive through the grace of God]. But I don't think for much longer, my child. Do you remember me? Ke mme wa Dineo Tau [I am the mother of Dineo Tau]. Remember, the little girl who was killed by the police? You wrote about it and landed in jail.

THANDEKA

Yes, yes, I still recognise you. It's been a long time.

ME'TAU

Yes.

THANDEKA

So, what can I do for you, Ma?

ME'TAU

My child, there is one more thing I have to do before I rest these weary bones. Re tswanetse go boloka ngwana wa rona ka tsela ya rona [We must bury our child in our ways]. I cannot rest until her soul ... and her bones are returned to the clan. I want you to help me find Dineo's remains so that we can give her a proper burial.

THANDEKA

Ma, no one knows where her body is or the bodies of thousands of others. The remains of unknown people are being discovered all over the land in shallow graves.

ME'TAU

But the men who killed her know where they buried her. How can you people hope to heal this land when there are so many restless souls roaming the land? Their spirits must come home.

[silence]

ME'TAU

I went to see one of the policemen that killed her. I went to his shop and he chased me away but I could see that he knew where my daughter is.

THANDEKA

Who did you go and see?

ME'TAU

The black one, called Dhlamini. It took me long to find him, just as long as it took me to find you.

THANDEKA

You went to see him?

ME'TAU

Yes, four times.

THANDEKA

Four times?

ME'TAU

Four times.

THANDEKA

What did he say?

ME'TAU

That I was confused ... He knew nothing. But when I told him that I was going to see you and that you and I are going to sort them out, he looked scared and warned me not to put my hand in a bee's nest. *[pleadingly]* We are going to bury her, won't we my child?

THANDEKA

Yes, yes mum ...

ME'TAU

Her soul and her bones must return to the clan; her spirit must come home.

ME'TAU stands up and walks out. As she leaves, with her back turned to **THANDEKA**, she breaks into a hymn, a powerful voice gushing forth out of her frail old body. **THANDEKA**, overcome with consternation, gets up from her chair and observes the departure of the old woman.

INTERLUDE D

ME'TAU's hymn continues to fill the air as **DINEO**, with **GREEN** in pursuit, runs past clothes hanging on a clothesline in the backyard of the church. Her run is interrupted by the **BLACK TOYOTA COROLLA**, which screeches to a stop a few metres behind her. The door of the **COROLLA** opens and a pair of boots emerges. **DINEO** sprints away and **GREEN**, calmly, follows her.

24 INT: SOWETO - KHUMALO RESIDENCE - BEDROOM - DAY

SIMANGALISO is engrossed in her bead project, which is spread on the bed on which she is sitting. As if performing some sacred ritual she threads beads, then glues on a few buttons and stars. She sculpts a piece of string into the shape of a heart. Finally she cuts out a paper heart, which she decorates and captions with the inscription 'This is a love letter'.

25 INT: SOWETO - SHEBEEN - NOON

THANDEKA enters a nondescript lounge with a number of patrons scattered about. Amongst the men are **BOUDA'D** and **LUCKY SITHOLE**, a black detective, who is playing pool on his own. **SITHOLE** greets her raucously.

THANDEKA

Hola, hola, hola.

SITHOLE

Ey, ey, look at this ghost from the past. Hey, T-man, what happened to you man?

THANDEKA

No, I'm around man, I'm around.

BOUDA'D

Hi, hi, the return of Django! Cowboys never die, die die by mistake! *[He shouts with excitement.]* Hola T-Man!

SITHOLE

T-Man! What did I do to you man that you must leave me with this lot, hey?

THANDEKA

What do you mean?

SITHOLE

I'm sick and tired of drinking with all these parasites. Look at that one, look at how thin he is.

BOUDA'D

Ah hey, Uncle.

THANDEKA

Aren't you supposed to be at work? What happened to your promise of 'zero tolerance' of crime?

SITHOLE

The work of a policeman is never done. That is why it is important to take a break. To tell you the truth, I do my best detective work while I am in here, looking at these ugly faces. They are so ugly they bring clarity to my thinking.

SITHOLE'S associates swear at him for his comments. The group is joined by the owner of the shebeen, **RAMY.**

THANDEKA

Bra Ramram's, howzit?

RAMY

Joining these moegoes [miscreants]?

THANDEKA

Mina [Me]? Never! Me, I'm just passing through. Some of us still remember that there's daai thing called a work ethic.

THANDEKA picks up **SITHOLE'S** drink and smells it.

SITHOLE

Hey, hey, los los [leave it, leave it].

THANDEKA

N'gaye i-juice da [Get me a juice, please].

RAMY

Themba, one glass of juice.

BOUDA'D

[teasing THANDEKA]

Do you hear the Bells, the Bells, they ringing?

THANDEKA

Hey, ngizokushaya. Ngizokushaya [I'll beat you up. I'll beat you up].

The others burst out laughing at **BOUDA'D's** suggestion that **THANDEKA** must buy Bell's Whisky. **THANDEKA** playfully picks up a cue and charges at **BOUDA'D.**

26 EXT: SOWETO - TOWNSHIP STREET IN FRONT OF SHEBEEN - NOON

THANDEKA and **BOUDA'D** are leaving the shebeen when **BOUDA'D** suddenly starts moving around like a praise poet ready to perform.

THANDEKA

Haai not now man, not now.

BOUDA'D

Ha T-man. Even Bishop Tutu says we must give praise where praise is due. *[He points at Thandeka as if he is conducting a choir.]* Vuthela umlilo sisi [Stoke the fire, my sister].

THANDEKA

[reciting]

Where does the breeze begin to blow, my brother?

BOUDA'D

[reciting]

I don't know, but where does the breeze begin to blow, my sister? *[He points at THANDEKA.]*

THANDEKA

Where does the breeze begin to blow, my brother?

BOUDA'D

[walking around THANDEKA with deliberate steps, as if stalking her]

They came at dawn for all the first-born male sons and they left only with you. So where does the breeze begin to blow, my sister?

[He starts laughing, then stops and looks pensively at THANDEKA.]

Fuck, T-man. It's that time of the year again man ... 28 days ... to our honeymoon. Fourteen years ago ... *[he makes a swooshing gesture to signal disappearance]* ... gone ... gone ... gone. You and I came back, T-man, so we can spook those bastards so they rot in jail ... and ... and check this out, nê, you and me, we sue the damn state for reparations. Reparations are a must, or else we look like fools in front of the Reconciliation Commission ... You and I, we will always remember him. Fuck reconciliation! We will freeze his face like a picture in our minds. Paah! *[He accompanies the word with a flick of his hand as if mimicking a camera flash going off.]*

BOUDA'D takes a decrepit looking wallet from his trouser pocket, opens it and takes out a neatly folded newspaper clipping: it is the famous picture of **DINEO** against the wall, her clenched fist raised.

BOUDA'D

The mother of all pictures! One click ... and all hell broke loose. All Mike wanted to be ... was a photographer and when he finally took the pic that mattered ... our lives were in tatters!

THANDEKA listens quietly and then deliberately opens her purse and gives **BOUDA'D** money.

BOUDA'D

Shot [Thanks], T-man. Sorry that you have to pay for my waters of Babylon! But I'd rather hear the Bells ringing in my glass than the wind blowing in my head! Can I tell you two secrets? Number one, those shits were fucking me up so bad, I wanted to tell them where you were but I didn't know. Number two ... they were fucking you up on the same farm they were fucking me up ... and they say the cops don't have a sense of humour.

THANDEKA

Bouda'd, would you be able to recognise the farm?

BOUDA'D

Fuck, T-man - I remember fockoll Joe, absolutely nothing. All I remember are the trees, man, that would go on forever and the breeze that would blow and blow and blow. Sharp T-man, ngizoku cava [I'll see you around] Joe.

THANDEKA gets into the **POLO**. Her attention is drawn to **THREE WOMEN**, all dressed in black, coming up the street. Two of the women are carrying a white chicken each, the third is pulling a goat. **THANDEKA** waits until they pass her and then drives off.

27 INT: CITY - SHOPPING MALL - MIDDAY

THANDEKA and **SIMANGALISO** are fooling around with sunglasses as they make their way to a **CASHIER** in a clothing store. They present their shopping to the **CASHIER**, who folds and rings up the blouses. The two leave the store, laughing, each carrying a brightly coloured shopping bag.

SIMANGALISO notices an abandoned shopping trolley. She places her bag in it and, excitedly, pushes it in front of **THANDEKA**. She then lunges to the front of the trolley, and perches precariously on the bottom panel of its frame, her upper body and hands bent over the top edges. With a naughty look, she beckons her mother to push her.

THANDEKA

You are not serious?

SIMANGALISO's naughty, pleading eyes tell her otherwise. **THANDEKA** places her bag in the trolley and jumps onto the back. The trolley darts down the mall's pedestrian walkway, sending both of them into peals of laughter. The two are soon admonished by a black **SECURITY GUARD**. On seeing the guard **THANDEKA** jumps off and stops the trolley. They grab their bags and run down an escalator.

28 INT: CITY - SHOPPING MALL - RESTAURANT - MIDDAY

THANDEKA and **SIMANGALISO**, with half-empty plates in front of them, are huddled together like two old girlfriends, recently united, in the middle of some serious gossip.

Occasionally **THANDEKA**, exuding a new confidence, signs a few words and then resorts to speaking. They are interrupted by a young **BOY** of **SIMANGALISO's** age, who walks up to the table and starts signing to **SIMANGALISO**. The **BOY** then says goodbye with a shy smile to both women and rejoins a **MAN**, who is standing next to the table, waiting for him.

THANDEKA

[looking at SIMANGALISO with a mischievous glint in her eyes]

What was that?

SIMANGALISO

[signing throughout]

Nothing.

THANDEKA

[mouthing and signing throughout]

How can a cute face like that be nothing?

SIMANGALISO

He is the brother of one of my friends ...

THANDEKA

He is the brother of your friend?

THANDEKA takes a piece of paper and a pen from her bag and writes, 'I enjoyed myself today'. **SIMANGALISO** smiles approvingly, then stops her mother from writing further. She indicates that **THANDEKA** should repeat the statement in sign language.

THANDEKA

What? No, no, no Mangi ... there's people! Today, myself, enjoyed. Today I enjoyed myself.

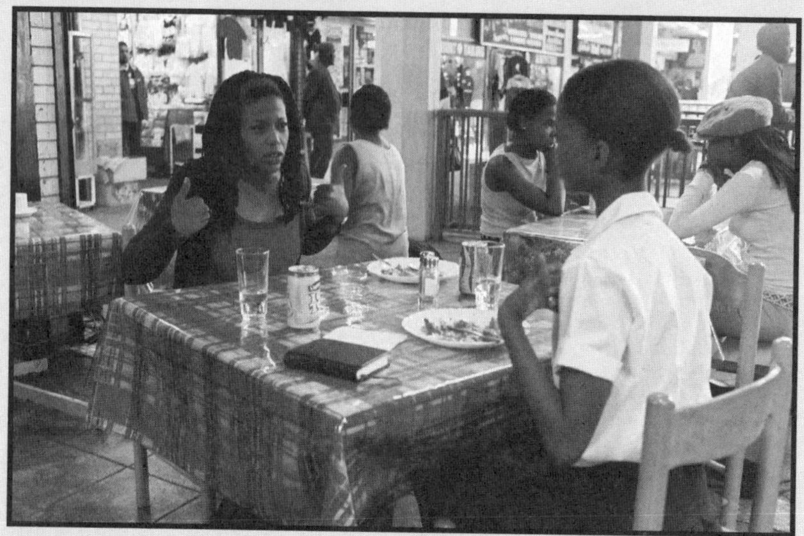

THANDEKA, suddenly awkward, tries to sign. **SIMANGALISO** corrects her mother's inept signing, patiently showing her how to do it: 'Today I've enjoyed myself.' **THANDEKA** finally gets it right.

[silence]

SIMANGALISO

Can I ask you a question?

THANDEKA

Since when do you need permission to ask me a question?

SIMANGALISO

It's just that I can't figure you out.

THANDEKA

You think I don't know what I want? What do you mean?

SIMANGALISO

Sipho?

THANDEKA

Sipho? What about him?

SIMANGALISO

What am I supposed to do with him?

THANDEKA

Who said you need to do anything with him?

SIMANGALISO

Well, he's the third guy you are seeing this year?

THANDEKA

You're counting the men in my life? I'm not counting and I don't see why you should!

SIMANGALISO

Because I have to adapt to them. You are not independent enough to live without a man.

THANDEKA

Mangi. You know so much and ... yet you know so little. Your father, he's a good man and loves you a lot ...

SIMANGALISO

I know that, it's you I can't figure out. Each time you seem to be reaching out to me ... it ends up with things just getting worse ...

THANDEKA

[cutting her short]

Yes, yes, I want to reach out to you. I'm ... I know, I know that I've said that before ... no more promises ... okay? I'll just have to redeem myself.

29 EXT: COUNTRYSIDE - MIDMORNING

The metallic blue **COROLLA** is speeding through the lush green countryside. The dust thrown up by the car's wheels on the gravel road is immediately swallowed up by the greenery and the endless trees standing like stubborn guards on the topography.

30 EXT: COUNTRYSIDE - FARMHOUSE - MIDMORNING

THANDEKA and **SIMANGALISO** are standing next to the wall of a veranda, watching doves pecking away under the shade of a tree.

THANDEKA

Look - doves. There used to be so many people in the townships with doves before things became so upside-down. When I was young, your granny used to tell beautiful stories about doves.

The two are startled by the voice of **MAKHUMALO**, who emerges around a corner of the house.

MAKHUMALO

[singing]

'Khoaba e khwetse hlapi molomong. Phokojwe a mo sheba ka takatso e kgolo. Phokojwe a re: "Ekare masiba a hao a matle le ho feta. Ntswe lona ke la kgeleke ka nnete. A nke o bine ke utlwe." Khoaba a ahlamisa molomo. Phokojwe ya phamola hlapi ya baleha [The crow had a fish in its beak and the jackal saw it and wanted the fish. Jackal then said to the crow, "You have such beautiful feathers and an even lovelier voice. Please sing for me." Without thinking, the crow started to sing and the fish fell out of its beak. The jackal ran away with the fish and the crow started to cry].'

SIMANGALISO hugs **MAKHUMALO** at the end of the old woman's narration.

31 EXT: COUNTRYSIDE - FARMHOUSE - MIDMORNING

THANDEKA is walking amongst the lush vegetation of the farm, her mind far away from the tranquillity that it encapsulates.

BOUDA'D

[off]

Where does the breeze begin to blow, my sister? Where does the breeze begin to blow? Where does the breeze begin to blow?

THANDEKA

[mumbling softly to herself]

Where does the breeze begin to blow?

BOUDA'D

[off]

I don't know.

THANDEKA

Where does the breeze begin to blow, my brother? Where ... the breeze ...

The repetition of the question is disrupted by fleeting images of a smiling **MICHAEL PETERS**.

INTERLUDE E

E 1

A tranquil country setting. A thick forest of trees frames a farmyard. There is a huge farmhouse on the left-hand side of the yard.

A vulture appears surreptitiously in the clear, midday blue sky. The tough but laboured flapping of its wings creates an eerie sound, similar to a human being's last gasps.

DHLAMINI is stoking a fire in front of the **BLACK TOYOTA COROLLA**, which is parked amid the shrubs. The car seems almost to be watching him.

E 2

A wheelchair stands on a dry patch of ground. **PETERS** sits impassively in the chair, his right hand massaging his right knee. His expression is peaceful. He turns and looks into the distance behind him. Less than two metres from him a huge fire, made from felled trees and wood, is crackling briskly in the heat of the midday sun. About three metres away meat is sizzling on a braai.

PETERS' attention is drawn to a movement at the northern end of the trees.

Three figures emerge: **MOOLMAN** and **DHLAMINI** are playing soccer, while **GREEN** is sitting next to a lake, engrossed in a magazine.

Suddenly **PETERS'** face starts to twitch with pain and within seconds his whole body goes into a cold sweat, shaking and shivering as foam starts to flow from his mouth. The convulsions throw him out of the wheelchair. His shaking body thunders against the dry soil, sending the vulture frantically into the sky: the sounds begin once more, marking the rhythm of the vulture's wings. **PETERS** is writhing on the ground. The vulture returns to the branch. **PETERS'** body goes still. The pastoral scene is tranquil once more.

GREEN closes the magazine and gets up. He is closely followed by **DHLAMINI** and **MOOLMAN**.

Walking past **PETERS'** comatose body **GREEN** goes to the braai, where he turns the meat over. **MOOLMAN** and **DHLAMINI** grab **PETERS** by the arms and drag him into the fire.

32 EXT: STREET IN FRONT OF TAU RESIDENCE - AFTERNOON

THANDEKA parks the **POLO** next to a wall in the **TAU's** barren yard, gets out of the car and enters the house.

33 INT: SOWETO - TAU RESIDENCE - AFTERNOON

THANDEKA awkwardly greets a number of **WOMEN** who are sitting on the floor of a room that has been cleared of all furniture. All the women are in black and there is a foreboding silence in the room.

THANDEKA stands in a corner of the room. Behind the slightly open door leading into the bedroom can be heard a male voice in the middle of a sermon.

PREACHER

KuHezekeli sizwa ukuthi abantu bakhala kuNkulunkulu, 'bethi amathambo abo omile, intanjana yempilo inqamukile'. Wenzile ke uNkulunkulu kuthi uHezekeli ahambehambe esigangeni awo amathambo a omile. Wayesephendula ke uNkulunkulu, ephendula uHezekeli ethi 'nginikeni amathambo abafileyo, ngizaphefumulela kuwona, aphile.' [In Ezekiel we hear that the people cried unto the lord saying, 'Our bones are dry, our thread of life is snapped'. The lord made Ezekiel to walk around the countless dry bones that littered the plain. Then God said to Ezekiel, 'Bring me the bones of the slain ... and I will breathe life into them. Bring me the bones of the slain ... and I will breathe life into them.'].

THANDEKA quietly edges her way into the kitchen and then to the backyard, where two younger **WOMEN**, one in her mid-twenties, the other about 14 years old, are washing dishes in an enamel washing basin.

THANDEKA

Dumelang. O teng mme [Hallo. Is your mother in]?

MAPULE, the 14-year-old, straightens up as she prepares to speak to **THANDEKA**.

MAPULE

E o teng. Ke tla ilo mitsa [She is inside. I'll go and call her].

THANDEKA

No, do not disturb her. I'll come back again. Ho etsahalang mo [What happened]?

MAPULE

It's a service that they have for my sister, Dineo, every month.

THANDEKA

Since a nyametse [Since she disappeared]?

[silence]

MAPULE

Sorry, a ke wena otlo thusang Ous' Dineo [Excuse me. Are you going to help find Dineo]?

[silence]

The women return to their chores. **THANDEKA** watches them for a moment and walks back to the **POLO**, going around the side of the house.

34 EXT: SOWETO - STREET IN FRONT OF TAU RESIDENCE - AFTERNOON

THANDEKA is standing next to the **POLO** absorbed in her thoughts.

The eerie calm of the street is suddenly disturbed when a small, decorated truck with a rudimentary sound system drives up the street. A group of people is standing on the open back of the truck trying to get the attention of whoever happens to be in the street. In the middle of the crew on the truck is **JONATHAN KHUBEKA**, the local councillor. He is flanked by two bodyguards.

KHUBEKA

Our people, come and witness the handing over of the first thousand houses to our people! Come and witness the proud work of a party that prides itself on speedy delivery of services to our people, our poor people.

The entourage disappears as **BOUDA'D** walks by with his pigeons.

35 INT: HILLBROW - STRIP CLUB - NIGHT

DHLAMINI walks into the club and quickly makes it clear to a prostitute at the entrance that he is here on business and not for pleasure. He scans the tables until he notices his former comrades. **GREEN** is ensconced between two black prostitutes. **DHLAMINI** whispers something to **MOOLMAN** and the two of them leave.

36 EXT: HILLBROW - STRIP CLUB - ROOF - NIGHT

DHLAMINI and **MOOLMAN** are standing on the roof of the club.

MOOLMAN

So, how's the shop doing?

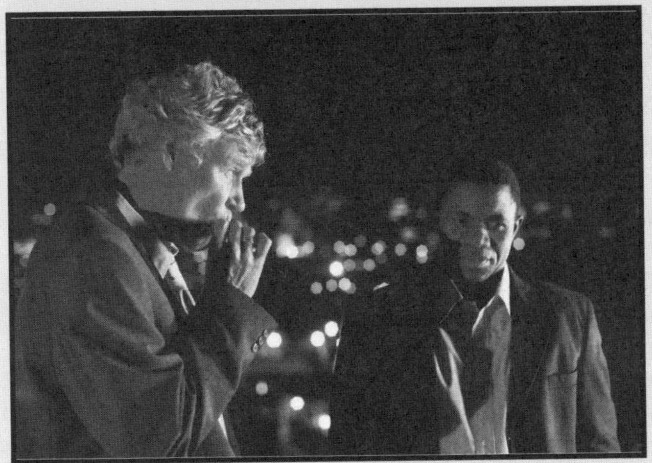

DHLAMINI

Okay ... nothing extraordinary, but ... ja ... okay. And the special services?

The two men watch **GREEN** climbing the stairs leading to the roof.

MOOLMAN

Why? You want to come back?

DHLAMINI

No, no.

GREEN

Ma se kind [my mother's child], long time no see. What brings you around?

DHLAMINI

There's this old lady and bitch who have been pestering me about the old lady's daughter.

MOOLMAN

Ag no, what? You made the daughter pregnant? Why don't you just pay lobola [dowry]!

DHLAMINI

I wish it was that simple. Look, she wants us to testify in front of the TRC [Truth and Reconciliation Commission] and tell them where we buried the body of her daughter. Do you remember the girl that we eliminated?

MOOLMAN

Which one? There were so many of them!

GREEN

'It is the cause, it is the cause, my soul.' 'The time is out of joint' '... things fall apart ...' 'I am my father's spirit ... doomed to walk the night' '... till the foul crimes done ... are burnt and purged away ...'

DHLAMINI

Look, I've got no time for your shit.

GREEN

Ma se kind [my mother's child], we are all in the

shit, it's the depth that varies. How did the woman find your place or did you find her first?

DHLAMINI

What are you insinuating?

GREEN

Big word, ma se kind, insinuate. I insinuate fokkol [nothing]. Or are you like the politicians and the generals ... prepared to sell out your own? Begging for mercy from the very communists that we are at war with?

MOOLMAN

Let's not get excited ...

GREEN

Shut up Moolie ... you now actually work for them. Let's get two things clear. One: I will not be testifying before any commission ... my sins I will only testify before God. Let's be absolutely clear about that. And two: everything I did was part of a calculated, methodological plan, researched and planned to the last detail, explained and accounted for in the ideology of the party from London to Cape Town to Washington, approved by the highest authorities in the land, and I have the medals to prove it! So, neither you, the Bishop, Madiba, or the courts are going to reduce me to being a maverick psychopath. Otherwise *[assumes melo-dramatic posture of pointing and shooting at each one of his associates]*, 'out, out brief candle'!

<u>37 INT: EIKENHOF - SEMI-RURAL AREA - AFTERNOON</u>

THANDEKA and **ME'TAU** are sitting quietly in the **POLO** as it speeds along a remote country road. The old woman directs **THANDEKA** to turn left at an intersection and immediately points towards a nondescript shop in the middle of nowhere, on the right-hand side of the road. The **POLO** stops next to the shop. The two women get out of the car and are confronted by a big sign that screams: **NEW AFRICAN GENERAL DEALERS**. They enter the shop.

38 INT: EIKENHOF - NEW AFRICAN GENERAL DEALERS - AFTERNOON

THANDEKA is hypnotised by the sparsely stocked shelves. Then the two women realise there is no one behind the counter.

ME'TAU

Hallo? Sanibonani? He's not here.

MADHLAMINI enters from a room adjoining the store and stands behind the counter.

MADHLAMINI

Sanibona [Good afternoon].

ME'TAU

Yebo.

MADHLAMINI

Ninjani [How are you]?

ME'TAU

Sikhona nina ninjani [Fine. And you]?

MADHLAMINI

Sikhona. Ngingani nceda [We are fine. Can I help you]?

ME'TAU

Sicela ukukhuluma noBaba [We would like to speak to the owner of the shop].

MADHLAMINI

Umyeni wami akekho [My husband is not here].

THANDEKA leaves the shop and goes outside.

ME'TAU

Uyazi kuthi uzofika nini [When do you expect him back]?

MADHLAMINI

Cha, angazi mpela [No, I don't know].

39 EXT: EIKENHOF - NEW AFRICAN GENERAL DEALERS - AFTERNOON

THANDEKA stands in the desolate landscape, clearly frustrated and tormented by the dust that is intermittently thrown up by the wind. She notices a group of three girls who are rehearsing a song. **SIBONGILE** and her **TWO FRIENDS** accompany their singing with synchronised hand movements. They stop their routine when they notice **THANDEKA** sitting and watching them.

THANDEKA

Nice.

SIBONGILE

Thank you. Sesikuma-provincial finals manje, uma siwina sizorepresenta i-region yethu eJohannesburg [We are in the provincial finals, if we win, we will represent our region in Johannesburg. You are from Johannesburg]?

THANDEKA

Yes, I am from Johannesburg.

SIBONGILE

Can we offer you a drink?

THANDEKA

Ngicela i-Coke [Can I have a Coke]?

40 INT: EIKENHOF - NEW AFRICAN GENERAL DEALERS - AFTERNOON

SIBONGILE

Ma, ngisalethela u-auntie isiphuzo [I am bringing a drink for aunty].

MADHLAMINI

Kulungile. Ngiyaxolisa, ifridji ayisebenzi futhi siphelelwe yi-ice. Kodwa ngizokupha yona, awuz' ukukhokha. Sibongile, lethela u-auntie i-ice [Pardon us, our fridge is not working and it's out of ice. Sibongile, fetch some ice].

The women are startled by the cry of a baby. **MADHLAMINI** disappears into the adjoining room and returns with the baby. **ME'TAU** follows **MADHLAMINI** and asks to see the child.

ME'TAU

oHa' ume kancani. 'Yizingane zikaDhlamini lezi? [Excuse me. Are these Dhlamini's children]?

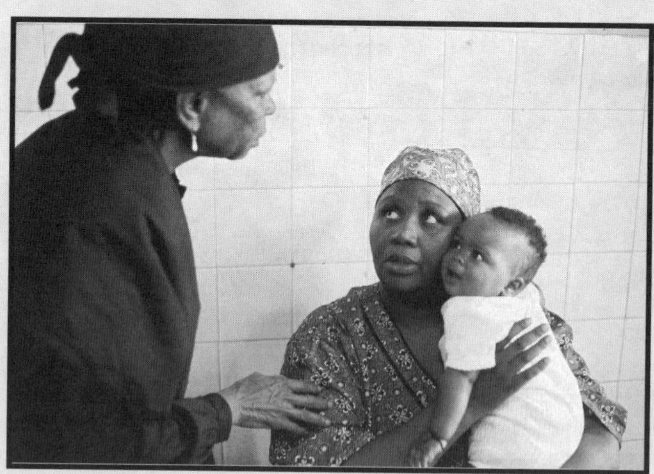

MADHLAMINI

Yebo [Yes].

ME'TAU is visibly distraught. **THANDEKA** notices **ME'TAU**'s change in demeanour and moves to her, trying to comfort her. **ME'TAU** turns away and goes out, leaving **THANDEKA** and **MADHLAMINI** behind.

THANDEKA

Tell him the old lady from Soweto was here. He knows who she is.

41 EXT: EIKENHOF - NEW AFRICAN GENERAL DEALERS - AFTERNOON

THANDEKA and **ME'TAU** are huddled together in a corner of the veranda of the shop.

ME'TAU

I've dreamt so much of this man and his friends. I never thought of him as anyone's father or husband. He's got children! Dineo also was a soloist in the church choir. Funny, she found politics at the church. She had such a powerful voice. She used to like to sing sad songs. *[singing]* 'When I am laid to earth ... buried in my grave, remember me! O nkgopole! Nkgopole [remember me. Remember me]!'

42 EXT: EIKENHOF - NEW AFRICAN GENERAL DEALERS - AFTERNOON

THANDEKA drives off. As the **POLO** leaves a green **MAZDA** arrives and stops next to the shop. **DHLAMINI** gets out and sees the choristers still hard at work. He joins them, frantically trying to keep up with their intricate steps. He is met by **SIBONGILE** and the two hug warmly before going into the shop.

43 INT: CITY - MAIL & GUARDIAN OFFICES - NIGHT

GREEN is rummaging through files stacked upright in a filing cabinet in Smith's office. He removes a file, which he places carefully on the desk. He pages through its contents until he finds a black-and-white picture of the killing of Dineo. **GREEN** closes the file and leaves the office. He stops next to Thandeka's desk, where he examines a picture of Thandeka, Moola and Simangaliso. **GREEN** moves around the desk and, opening a drawer, takes out a folder. In it he finds portraits of Moolman, Dhlamini and himself.

44 INT: SOWETO - KHUMALO RESIDENCE - LOUNGE - AFTERNOON

THANDEKA, MAKHUMALO and **SIMANGALISO** are sitting at a small wooden table with a bowl of beads in front of them. The hands of the three generations of the Khumalo family silently weave beads into Mangi's bead project. There is an air of serenity, beauty and regeneration.

45 EXT: SOWETO - STREET - AFTERNOON

THANDEKA is driving slowly through a throng of people: men, women, young and old, sick and well, who are walking in the same direction. As the **POLO** turns a corner, more people seem to be on the same journey. Many are carrying banners emblazoned with statements like **'IXESHA LOKUTHETHA INYANISO NGOKHU [IT IS TIME TO TELL THE TRUTH]'** and **'THEY LOST THEIR LIVES'**. There are hundreds of people ahead, walking in long lines that snake their way into the distance. Most of the elderly women are dressed in black, as is **ME'TAU**.

ME'TAU

Emisa koloi mona ngwanaka. Ke kopa ho tsamaya le batho bana [Stop the car, I want to walk with the people].

THANDEKA

Okay.

THANDEKA, clearly perplexed, stops the **POLO** on a pavement. She locks the car and joins **ME'TAU** and the crowd. In front of them a MAN in his mid-thirties is sitting in a wheelbarrow being pushed by a **WOMAN**. Behind them is a **YOUNG MAN** in his early twenties: he is blind and is being led by a friend. A number of people are in wheelchairs. As the crowd weaves its way **THANDEKA** notices posters nailed to poles and attached to fences all the way down the street:

'TRUTH AND RECONCILIATION COMMISSION'

'REGISTRATION: BREAK THE SILENCE'

'STOP BEING A VICTIM!'

46 EXT: SOWETO - SCHOOL HALL - LATE AFTERNOON

The light slowly fades as the night beckons, but in the hall hundreds are still standing in line, waiting to reach one of the dozens of tables where clerks are recording people's details. **KHUBEKA** is wandering around, talking to people and shaking the hands of some. **THANDEKA** and **ME'TAU** are in a line. **THANDEKA** removes her cellphone from her bag and dials.

THANDEKA

Hey, Moola, it's me. Look, I'm not going to be able to fetch Mangi. Please get her for me. If you don't call I'll assume you've got this message. Okay, bye.

47 EXT: NORTHERN SUBURBS - ST MARY'S SCHOOL GROUNDS - EARLY EVENING

SIMANGALISO, in school uniform, is sitting, forlornly, on a wooden bench in a courtyard in front of the entrance to the school's administrative block. **A NUN** comes out of the building and notices her. She walks deliberately towards the young girl and enquires why she has not been fetched. She takes **SIMANGALISO's** hand and leads her inside.

48 INT: NORTHERN SUBURBS - ST MARY'S SCHOOL - DORMITORY - NIGHT

SIMANGALISO, wearing long cotton pyjamas, is standing intently in front of a bed. She looks at her classmates, who are sleeping soundly. She slowly walks out of the dormitory.

INTERLUDE F

F 1

SIMANGALISO is in the school's science laboratory, standing in front of the sinks. She stares fixedly at the two taps and, almost immediately, water starts to run out of them.

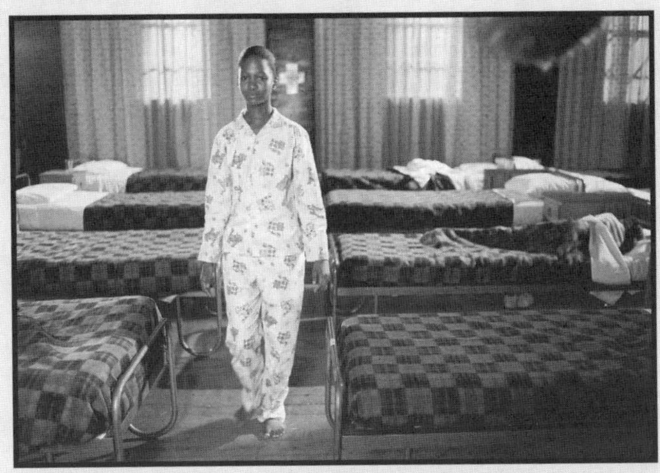

F 2

SIMANGALISO is sitting in the lotus position in the middle of a passage. Streams of water are flooding the corridor and making their way towards her. Her fragile face shows that she has been crying. Soon her tears will be washed away.

49 INT: HILLBROW - THANDEKA'S FLAT - BEDROOM - NIGHT

THANDEKA is sitting on the edge of her bed talking into a phone. **SIPHO**, hunched on his elbows, is next to her.

THANDEKA

Look, I am sorry ... Moola ...

Noticing **SIPHO**'s inappropriate proximity, she moves onto the carpeted floor. Insulted by her need for privacy **SIPHO** gets up and leaves.

THANDEKA

Just listen to your answering machine. I left a message earlier. When you didn't call I thought you had it covered. Is she sleeping? Thanks ... goodnight. Moola, I'm really sorry. Okay. Bye. *[She puts the receiver down.]* Shit!

THANDEKA covers herself with a shawl and goes out onto the balcony.

50 EXT: HILLBROW - THANDEKA'S FLAT - BALCONY - NIGHT

THANDEKA stands on the balcony, peering at the dark contours of the Johannesburg skyline. After a while it seems she has resolved some dilemma and she turns, drops the shawl and goes back into the flat.

51 EXT: LENASIA - STREET IN FRONT OF MOOLA'S HOUSE - NIGHT

THANDEKA is struggling to climb over the gate at **MOOLA**'s house. She finally manages to scale the wall, jumps and lands on her feet before tumbling over. She rises slowly, picks up a bottle of whisky, dusts herself off and staggers towards the front door. After a while, lights are switched on in the interior of the house.

52 INT: LENASIA - MOOLA'S HOUSE - NIGHT

THANDEKA walks down the passage leading to **SIMANGALISO**'s bedroom. She enters the room and looks at her sleeping daughter. The bead project has been flung carelessly on the bed. Satisfied, **THANDEKA** turns around. **MOOLA** follows her into the lounge.

MOOLA

Thandi, we really need to get some sleep. Give me your car keys and I'll bring your car in. Okay?

THANDEKA

Okay, but ... did you get my message ...

MOOLA

Yes.

THANDEKA

Don't lie to me! Where is the cell?

THANDEKA moves around the lounge looking for the cellphone.

THANDEKA

I know you don't believe me. Look at your face, as smug as all the others ... the high and mighty ... Well this time I am telling the truth. I left a message saying I was stuck at the school, can you fetch Mangi. Now where is the damn phone?

She finds the phone on a cabinet.

THANDEKA

Is this thing on? I am sick and tired of people standing in judgement over me ... like I don't love my child. I love my girl, do you hear me, Mr Excellent Father ... Mr 'I will always be there for my Girl'? Well, have I got news for you! Where were you when I found out that I was pregnant? Were you here? Hell no! Halfway across the bloody globe searching for your roots in India. Well, fuck

India, fuck you and fuck the whole bunch of self-righteous shits that are on my neck. [*She has retrieved the message.]* Listen ...

MOOLA

[exasperated]

I told you I listened to the message after you explained to me what had happened.

THANDEKA

Who cares?

Exhausted, **THANDEKA** plumps herself down on a couch.

THANDEKA

How I wish Mike had been at the school today. The people looked so weary. Mike knew how to make people look beautiful. His wedding photos ... on lush green lawns ... migrant workers standing next to water fountains ... skyscrapers of Johannesburg behind them; sentimental, colourful pictures to send to the folks back home: we are still alive. Mike would still be making beauty for some dreamers ... if, if I had not taken him to the Mail & Guardian.

THANDEKA breaks down and cries uncontrollably.

53 INT: HILLBROW - THANDEKA'S FLAT - DININGROOM - EVENING

THANDEKA is dishing up food while **SIMANGALISO**, in pyjamas, plays a hand-held computer game. The silence between the two is interrupted intermittently by the irritating noise made by the game. **THANDEKA** finally takes the game away from **SIMANGALISO**.

THANDEKA

Mangi, eat, baby, come on.

THANDEKA sits down and looks at **SIMANGALISO**, who is scraping the bottom of her plate with her spoon.

THANDEKA

[signing]

Mangi, Mangi, Mangi stop ... please, just eat, okay? Look, I said I was sorry. Something unexpected happened. Mangi, please, speak to me. Speak!

SIMANGALISO suddenly pushes her food away, rises and confronts her mother.

SIMANGALISO

[signing and also painfully trying to vocalise her words]

What I don't understand is why you want to change the world ... when you can't change the situation in your own family.

THANDEKA is shocked.

THANDEKA

[furious]

Change what situation in my family? You are not the only person in this world who is in need! You never ever speak to me like that again! Do you hear me!

SIMANGALISO

[pointing to herself]

Deaf!

THANDEKA and **SIMANGALISO** stare at each other, stunned by the altercation. **SIMANGALISO** storms out of the room. **THANDEKA** clasps her head in both hands and waits until she regains her composure. Embarrassed and ashamed, she follows **SIMANGALISO**. The food remains on the table, untouched.

54 INT: THANDEKA'S FLAT - HILLBROW - BEDROOM - NIGHT

THANDEKA finds **SIMANGALISO** sitting on her bed, clutching a pillow. **THANDEKA** sits next to her.

THANDEKA

[part signing, part talking]

Mangi, I'm sorry.

[silence]

After a while **THANDEKA** leaves the room, full of remorse.

55 INT: THANDEKA'S FLAT - HILLBROW - DININGROOM - NIGHT

The room and furniture are in silhouette, illuminated by faint streams of light spilling in from outside. **SIMANGALISO** gets out of bed and walks into **THANDEKA's** bedroom. The bed is empty. **SIMANGALISO** finds her mother sleeping, fully dressed on the couch in the living room, a notebook on her lap.

SIMANGALISO bends and opens the folder that is lying on the floor next to the couch. She scans its contents and pulls out a number of photos. They include the famous picture of Dineo and a profile of Peters. She looks at the pictures and then carefully returns everything to the folder.

SIMANGALISO's attention is suddenly drawn to the glass door leading to the balcony. There is an image of her on the door.

Interlude G

G 1

SIMANGALISO walks towards the door, which suddenly opens, and her image disappears. A gust of wind rises and seems to suck her towards the balcony. Suddenly, all around her the papers from **Thandeka's** folder are swept outside onto the balcony and into the air.

G 2

SIMANGALISO steps out onto the balcony and is lifted over the barrier.

G 3

SIMANGALISO is airborne, flying with her arms outstretched. A flock of white pigeons flies around her.

G 4

SIMANGALISO is walking over the veld towards a small group of people. The group, dressed colourfully in traditional attire, is singing and dancing, celebrating a wedding.

ENTOURAGE

Woza makoti, sikulandile [Bride, come with us].

In the middle of the crowd is the bridal couple, their backs turned towards the advancing **SIMANGALISO**. The bride turns around and looks at **SIMANGALISO**: it is **THANDEKA**. **THANDEKA** lifts her right hand and is waving at the advancing **SIMANGALISO** when gunshots echo through the hills, scattering the wedding crowd. **THANDEKA** is left alone. She takes one last look at her daughter and then evaporates as the figures of **GREEN**, **MOOLMAN** and **DHLAMINI** emerge from the grass of the veld.

56 INT: THANDEKA'S FLAT - LOUNGE - MORNING

THANDEKA enters and finds **SIMANGALISO** working on the laptop in the living room.

THANDEKA

Thank you for tidying up.

SIMANGALISO

No problem.

THANDEKA

Okay, come on. We have to go.

THANDEKA closes the balcony door.

THANDEKA

Mangi, come on. Let's go ... come.

SIMANGALISO

Mama, mama will you testify before the TRC?

THANDEKA

Yes.

SIMANGALISO

On your behalf?

THANDEKA

No, no, no, sit. You remember, the old lady that we picked up?

SIMANGALISO

Me'Tau?

THANDEKA

Me'Tau, yes.

SIMANGALISO

I read the file last night ...

THANDEKA

You read this file? You looked at this? Well, you shouldn't have. Me'Tau wants to appear before the TRC.

SIMANGALISO

Did you know her daughter?

THANDEKA

Yes, I knew her daughter.

SIMANGALISO

And the three men?

THANDEKA

Oh no, no. They are not worth knowing. Come, let's go.

SIMANGALISO

Mama. You won't request a hearing?

THANDEKA

And achieve what?

SIMANGALISO

I don't know ...

THANDEKA

Nothing can compensate me for what I went through. And there is no talk of either arresting them or paying the abused families.

SIMANGALISO

What did you go through?

THANDEKA

Mangi, please. Not now.

SIMANGALISO

When? When will you tell me what you went through. And the three men ... *[She mimes someone shooting.]* I'm afraid ...

SIMANGALISO leaves and **THANDEKA** remains rooted on the spot.

57 INT: THANDEKA'S FLAT - HILLBROW - BEDROOM - DAY

THANDEKA and **SIMANGALISO** are sitting on SIMANGALISO's bed, the bead project between them. They explore the many pockets, the pictures and the notes as though they are unravelling a puzzle. **SIMANGALISO** takes out the note with 'This is a love letter' written on it. **THANDEKA** takes it, then whispers and signs 'I love you too'.

58 INT: SOWETO - KHUMALO RESIDENCE - KITCHEN - MIDMORNING

THANDEKA is tasting the food she is cooking. Pots are bubbling on the stove.

59 INT: SOWETO - KHUMALO RESIDENCE - DININGROOM - NOON

The KHUMALO family is about to start eating the Sunday lunch prepared by **THANDEKA**. **THANDEKA** has changed into smart-casual attire.

THANDEKA

Okay ... feast time!

MAKHUMALO

Time for feasting.

BAB'KHUMALO

Siyabonga-ke Thandi, mntanami [Ah, we are thankful, Thandi my child].

MAKHUMALO

He babaka Thandi, waze wayidonsa umfundisi uMaphumulo ikhonzo ... [The priest really stretched his sermon today].

BAB'KHUMALO

Uyazi - ke, kufuneka abafundisi bazi kuthi they must always go straight to the point, especially uma kukhona izinto ezinjengalezi ekhaya [Priests must learn to go straight to the point, especially when there is still unfinished business at home]. Let's have a toast for a nice day.

60 EXT: SOWETO - KHUMALO RESIDENCE - AFTERNOON

THANDEKA escorts her family to the car as they leave for an afternoon visit. As soon as the **VALIANT** drives off she notices a commotion down the street involving **BOUDA'D** and two black **POLICEMEN. BOUDA'D** gesticulates wildly as a **POLICEMAN** tries to grab his arm. **THANDEKA** runs to the scene.

THANDEKA

Hey, hey, yini 'smoko [What's the problem]?

POLICEMAN ONE

A kuna smoko. Siyasebenza [There's no problem here. We are working].

BOUDA'D

Mosono wa'o maan [Your arse man]!

POLICEMAN ONE

O reng? O reng [What did you say]?

BOUDA'D

These bastards say my inoculation mark is too low. Fuck you, where's your one?

POLICEMAN ONE

I'll lock you up, okay?

BOUDA'D

Fuck T-man. Imagine if some nurse suffering from a hangover twenty year ago inoculated you here ... *[pointing to a spot on his arm]* then you are seen as someone who is from Mozambique. Fuck off man. This shit is deep.

61 EXT: SOWETO – STREET IN FRONT OF TAU RESIDENCE – EARLY EVENING

DHLAMINI, deep in thought, sits in his **MAZDA** opposite the Tau house. He stares at the house, motionless and silent. His eyes come alive when he sees **ME'TAU** come out of the house to empty a bucket of water. She notices the car, stops her activity and rushes back inside.

62 EXT: SOWETO – STREET IN FRONT OF TAU RESIDENCE – EVENING

DHLAMINI is sitting in the car looking crestfallen.

VOICE

[from the tape in the car]

It is in the Song of Solomon that we find the most beautiful ode to life, to living, and love.

DHLAMINI lifts his burdened face and repeats in a tormented tone, just a beat behind, the lines narrated on the cassette.

VOICE

'My lover has gone down to his gardens, to the beds of the spices, and browse in the gardens and gather lilies. I am my lover's and my lover is mine; he browses among the lilies.'

63 EXT: SOWETO - STREET IN FRONT OF TAU RESIDENCE - EVENING

DHLAMINI pensively smokes a cigarette. He gets out of the **MAZDA** and walks towards the Tau house.

64 INT: SOWETO - TAU RESIDENCE - LOUNGE - EVENING

ME'TAU and **MAPULE** are staring anxiously out of a window, their eyes fixed on the MAZDA parked across the street. They see the driver's door open and **DHLAMINI** emerge. They watch DHLAMINI's pacing with consternation.

65 EXT: SOWETO - STREET IN FRONT OF TAU RESIDENCE - EVENING

DHLAMINI finally comes to some decision. He returns to his car and drives off.

66 INT: HILLBROW - THANDEKA'S FLAT - BEDROOM - EVENING

THANDEKA is sitting on her bed watching a video demonstration of how to sign. She watches intently and starts to replicate and repeat some of the words she is learning, mouthing and signing as if to guide herself in her new challenge. She finally turns away from the television and, like a child performing to herself, repeats the words and gestures.

The doorbell rings and the lights linked to the bell flicker. **THANDEKA** gets up and makes her way to the door where she finds an A4 envelope lying on the floor. She immediately opens the door, peers over the banisters and hears the front door of the block of flats close. She returns to the flat.

67 INT: HILLBROW - THANDEKA'S FLAT - BEDROOM - EVENING

THANDEKA opens the envelope, takes out its contents and puts them on the bed, but is distracted by the sound of a car starting up. She rushes to the window and hears the car drive off. She closes the curtains and returns to sit on the bed where a picture of Peters is lying. She sits staring at the picture, distraught.

INTERLUDE H

H 1

THANDEKA and **PETERS** are sprinting between the pews in the church. They take cover at a window where they see **DINEO** about to be shot. **THANDEKA** grimaces in pain.

H 2

As the **POLO** navigates a corner it is suddenly faced with the blue flashing lights of a police and army roadblock. **POLICE OFFICERS** and **SOLDIERS** are spread around the intersection. Some of the **POLICE** are in the process of searching a BMW parked on the opposite side of the road. Two black MEN in their twenties are lying on the sandy ground, face down, their arms handcuffed behind their backs.

POLICEMEN walk towards the POLO. The leader of the unit flashes his torch into the open windows and the squinting faces of the passengers.

POLICEMAN

Good evening ma'am. Will you please hand me your driver's licence and will you get out of the car for me please?

THANDEKA obliges. The **COPS** inspect the interior of the car. They are done in seconds and wave her on. **THANDEKA** drives past the two young **MEN** lying, handcuffed, on the ground.

H 3

The **POLO** speeds along eerily dark, haunting, swirling township streets. **THANDEKA** seems to be in a dream-like state, searching desperately for someone in the area. She drives past the lonely figure of **ME'TAU** standing in the street screaming her daughter's name.

ME'TAU

Dineo! Dineo!

H 4

A helicopter with a searchlight hovers above the **POLO**, tracking it down as it tries to speed away. The **POLO** comes to a sudden stop. Its doors burst open and **DINEO** jumps out and sprints down the dark, deserted street. **THANDEKA** leaps out of the car, screaming to **DINEO** to come back.

THANDEKA

Dineo! Dineo!

DINEO's feet, in full flight, take over the screen.

H 5

DINEO's feet give way under her and she crashes to the ground, the church framing the night skyline behind her. As she struggles to get up the figure of an assassin comes into view: he is carrying a gun in his left hand. Shots ring out in staccato and **DINEO** stumbles again.

[silence]

THANDEKA watches as **DINEO** looks back at her before **DINEO** gently slides to the ground.

68 EXT: SOWETO - STREET IN FRONT OF TAU RESIDENCE - MORNING

THANDEKA brings the **POLO** to a stop next to **ME'TAU's** house. She alights and meets **ME'TAU** in the front yard, which **ME'TAU** is sweeping.

THANDEKA

Dumela [Good morning], Ma.

ME'TAU

I did not sleep last night. I hope you can find it in your heart to forgive me. We must go back and cancel my testimony.

THANDEKA

Why, Ma, what happened?

ME'TAU turns and moves towards the back of the house. There they find **MAPULE** sitting on the side of the stairs in front of the door.

THANDEKA

What happened?

MAPULE

The policeman that picked up my sister was here again yesterday.

THANDEKA

How many of them? Is that why you're not in school?

MAPULE simply nods.

[silence]

MAPULE

Ke kopa o buwe le Mme [Please talk to my mother] ... we can't turn back now ... I mean I can't take it anymore, I just can't take living in this house full of mourning and sadness, can't live in a house with a permanent wake.

THANDEKA

You know why your mother's concerned, don't you? Your sister's story is my story ... It is the story of so many families and so is the courage and love that you have shown. I've been meaning to testify myself. You want to end the wake in the house ... I need to end the wake in my head. I've written and said so much about what is happening around me. Now I need to write about what's happened to me. This thing ... it is so big, so frightening, and no one knows where it will lead. Your mother is scared that if she goes through with this she will lose you. I'm scared that if I don't go through with this, I will lose myself ... and Simangaliso.

THANDEKA leaves.

69 EXT: SOWETO – KHUMALO'S RESIDENCE – NIGHT

MOOLA and **SIMANGALISO** come out of the house, escorted by the elderly couple. A strong wind is blowing. The grandparents wave them off as the car departs.

A few seconds later a **BAKKIE** pulls off from the opposite side of the road and follows the **COROLLA**.

69 B

MOOLA notices the **BAKKIE** behind him, trying to overtake him, its bright lights reflecting on the inside mirror and blinding him. He slows down and waits for the **BAKKIE** to pass. It does not pass but slows down and falls in behind him again.

MOOLA looks across and sees that the **BAKKIE** is again trying to overtake. The two cars run parallel for a moment before **MOOLA**, sensing that something is amiss, decides to accelerate.

69 C

The gap between the two cars has narrowed again. Fear is etched on **SIMANGALISO's** face as she watches, through the rear window, the **BAKKIE** about to ram into the back of the **COROLLA**.

70 EXT: SOWETO – STREET – SCENE OF ACCIDENT – NIGHT

THANDEKA arrives at the scene of the accident and is met by Detective **LUCKY SITHOLE**.

SITHOLE

It's okay, it's okay, take it easy.

THANDEKA

[on seeing the carnage]

No. No. Oh my God, no. No. No.

SITHOLE

Easy, easy, easy, T-man.

SITHOLE guides her to the body of **MOOLA** in a body bag. At the sight of the body **THANDEKA** gets hysterical. **SITHOLE** grabs her and tries to console her. When the body is removed by policemen **THANDEKA** breaks free from **SITHOLE** and confronts a **WHITE COP.** She slaps him and shoves him around.

THANDEKA

[raging]

No! You bastards! You are the ones responsible for this. Where is my child? Where is my daughter? Where is she? Where is she?

The **WHITE COP** parries her jabs. **SITHOLE** pulls her away.

SITHOLE

We'll find her, T-man! We'll find her.

THANDEKA

Where is my baby? Where is my baby? Where is she? Where is my child?

THANDEKA notices **SIMANGALISO**'s rucksack lying on the ground. There are beads spilled around it. She crawls to the bag.

THANDEKA

[muttering to herself]

Where is my baby? Where is my baby? Where is she? Where is my child? Mangi! Where is my baby? Where is my baby?

THANDEKA picks up the rucksack and, as though in a daze, looks to the heavens for assistance.

THANDEKA

Mangi! Mangi! Mangi!!

SITHOLE

We'll find her, T-man! We'll find her, T-man!

71 EXT: SOWETO – STREET – NIGHT

SIMANGALISO, tired, is jogging along a deserted street.

72 EXT: SOWETO – NIGHT

THANDEKA is driving through the streets of Soweto. She goes through a number of intersections and then brings the car to a sudden stop, turns it around and speeds across an intersection.

73 EXT: SUBURB ON THE OUTSKIRTS OF SOWETO – NIGHT

THANDEKA brings the **POLO** to a halt in front of the high walls of a house in a plush Soweto suburb. She gets out of the car and runs to the gate, where she rings the bell and speaks into an intercom.

THANDEKA

Hey, I need to see Councillor Khubeka.

GUARD

[off]

You can't see him.

THANDEKA

Fuck!

THANDEKA runs to the POLO and leans on the hooter, shattering the peace of the neighbourhood.

THANDEKA

[her eyes fixed on the gate]

Come on! Come on!

The gate opens and **THANDEKA** is confronted by two **SECURITY GUARDS**. She returns to the gate.

THANDEKA

Is Councillor Khubeka here?

GUARD ONE

Who wants to know?

THANDEKA

Okay.

She turns as though she is returning to her car but suddenly turns back and, with immense force, runs past the two **GUARDS** and into the yard with the **GUARDS** in hot pursuit.

THANDEKA

[screaming]

Khubeka! Khubeka!

Interlude I

I 1

THANDEKA is scratching against the rough walls of an austere, makeshift prison cell. She is rolling on a mattress lying on the ground. She is in agony, clutching at her stomach and other parts of her body in desperation.

74 EXT: SUBURB ON THE OUTSKIRTS OF SOWETO - NIGHT

THANDEKA is held to the ground by the **GUARDS** while she continues to scream **KHUBEKA's** name. The door to the house opens and **KHUBEKA** emerges.

KHUBEKA

Kwenzakalani la? Myekeni. Myekeni. [Hey, what's happening here? Let her go]! And what the hell do you think you are doing?

THANDEKA

Well, you are supposed to be my councillor, aren't you?

KHUBEKA

But that does not give you the damn right to barge in here and scare the shit out of my family.

THANDEKA

Oh, your family ... fuck your family. Well at least they are safe inside that house.

KUBHEKA

My sister, if I could help ...

THANDEKA

Then bring me my child ... and I want the men who killed her father to be brought here to me.

KHUBEKA

How possible is that?

THANDEKA

You were an activist. You were detained. How is it that we now see nothing, feel nothing, when all around us the misery continues?

KHUBEKA

I ... look, I get you, my sister.

THANDEKA

We are supposed to be in charge in this country. You are supposed to be my testimony to the fact that you and I have finally triumphed. It's not me that you are supposed to get ... it is them you are supposed to get!

KHUBEKA

Look, you know, the truth will out my sister.

THANDEKA

Fuck the truth. The only truth I know is what I felt with my entire body. I know that floor, the exact measurements of that cell ...

Interlude I

I 2

The bars of a prison door open and take the eye on a tour of its interior. Through the single window the dense trees on a farm are seen.

75 EXT: SUBURB ON THE OUTSKIRTS OF SOWETO - NIGHT

THANDEKA is engrossed in her account to KUBHEKA.

THANDEKA

Five months and three days ... enough time to see and feel the four walls of the cell even when you are fast asleep. And all the time, inside here, each kick, each movement, from a child as stubborn as her mother ... scared the shit out of me. Do I tell them of the life inside of me? Will it bring me mercy? Or will it bring new pleasures to the beatings? When she was born deaf ... *[With a sense of resignation]* Excuse me ... I have a child to bring up.

THANDEKA turns and makes her way towards her car.

KHUBEKA

Look, you can give me all the details and I'll personally ensure that the person you suspect is brought to book.

76 INT: HILLBROW - THANDEKA'S BLOCK OF FLATS - UNDERGROUND GARAGE - NIGHT

THANDEKA's head is pressed against the steering wheel of the POLO. After a while she rocks back against the seat, clutching her face. She has been crying. She gets out of the car and makes her way to her flat. The silence of the night is disturbed by the sound of her footsteps and gasping breath.

77 INT: HILLBROW – THANDEKA'S BLOCK OF FLATS – UNDERGROUND GARAGE – NIGHT

THANDEKA is walking up the stairs leading to her flat. She opens the door and enters, clutching **SIMANGALISO's** bag.

78 INT: HILLBROW – THANDEKA'S FLAT – NIGHT

THANDEKA pours herself a glass of water and steps out onto the balcony.

79 EXT: HILLBROW – THANDEKA'S FLAT – BALCONY – NIGHT

THANDEKA, somewhat refreshed, is searching the city's skyline. She remains transfixed by its dazzling lights for some time. After a while, she notices **SIMANGALISO** sitting on the ground, fast asleep, leaning against the gate leading to the balcony. **THANDEKA** rushes and kneels at the gate, whispering **SIMANGALISO's** name, scared to touch her or to wake her up.

THANDEKA

Mangi! Mangi! My baby!

She finally plucks up the courage to caress **SIMANGALISO's** face gently. **SIMANGALISO** wakes up, sees her mother, and the two instinctively embrace.

SIMANGALISO

Mama! Mama!

Weeping tears of relief and joy, the two touch each other's faces as if each is making sure the other is really there.

80 INT: HILLBROW - THANDEKA'S FLAT - BEDROOM - NIGHT

THANDEKA is sitting on the floor at the foot of **SIMANGALISO**'s bed. **SIMANGALISO** is fast asleep. The light in the room is dim, casting warm shadows. **THANDEKA** is mending elements of the bead project. After a while she picks up one of the pockets and opens it, revealing a photo of **MOOLA** and **SIMANGALISO** with the inscription: 'I LOVE YOU'.

81 EXT: COUNTRYSIDE - OPEN FARMLAND - DAY

THANDEKA is resting against a fallen tree trunk on the farm on which she and PETERS were detained. The strains of a hymn are heard in the background. After gathering herself she returns to a group of people, all dressed in black, about to begin a cleansing ritual. She joins **MAPULE**, **MAKHUMALO**, **BAB'KHUMALO**, **SIMANGALISO**, **BOUDA'D** and relatives huddled together in the middle of a clearing, framed by huge trees.

In the middle of the circle is an enamel basin filled with water and aloes. A broom made of leaves is bobbing on top of the water. Slightly in front of them is **ME'TAU** with four other WOMEN, all mothers of slain children. With their heads slightly bowed they are listening intently to a **PRIEST**, who is flanked by two young **ACOLYTES.**

PRIEST

Re e fumane 'nete, hore mo ke mo ditopi ditjhesitsweng teng ha bohloko. Ke tse kae? A re itse. Se re se itseng ke gore sebaka sa madi a tsholohileng teng mo a tlamegile gore a hlapiwe [It has been confirmed that this is the spot where their bodies were burnt beyond recognition. How many? We don't know. We do know that because of the blood that has been spilled here, this place must be cleansed].

KHUBEKA and a delegation of **POLICE**, some in plain clothes, others in uniform, are standing apart from the group, watching the ceremony.

ACTIVIST

Bafowethu nodadewethu abalele kulendawo, sizohlala njalo sinikhumbula. Namhlanje sizonilanda ukuba nihambe nathi siye ekhaya. Siyabonga [Our brothers and sister who are buried here, we will always remember you. We have come to fetch you so that we can return home. We thank you for your sacrifice].

MOTHER ONE enters the circle, takes the broom from the bucket and, with sweeping movements in the air, sprays drops of water on to the soil as she communicates with the departed.

MOTHER ONE

Bana ba rona, re tlo tla lelata kajeno hore le ye hae. Re a tseba hore le shwetse ntweng. Le ile la re shwela, la re lwanela. Kajeno etlong, e yang mahabo lona kaofela ha lona [Our children we've come to fetch you today so that you can return home. You died in battle, you sacrificed yourselves].

MOTHER TWO

Re tlo lelata masole a South Afrika. Le re lwanetse, ha re yeng hae [Warriors who died for our freedom, let's return home].

THANDEKA ushers **ME'TAU** forward and she takes the broom.

ME'TAU

Bana beso, a re kgutleleng hae. A re kgutleleng moo le tswaletsweng teng. Meloko le metswalle, le baruti ba le emetse. Isikhati sifikile, asiyini emakhaya [My children, come and let us go home. Let us return to where you were born, where your relatives, friends, teachers are waiting for you. It is time to go home].

ME'TAU returns the broom to the basin as the group breaks into another hymn.

81 INT: SOWETO - TAU RESIDENCE - BEDROOM - NIGHT

THANDEKA and **SIMANGALISO**, together with the rest of the entourage, are participating in a cleansing ceremony marked by a deep sense of ritual and colour. The floor in the small room has been transformed into a sacred arena. The PRIEST is seated to the right of the shrine. A huge calabash, filled with traditional beer, occupies the centre space on top of a cowhide. Just behind the calabash is a picture of Dineo, between a mesmerising array of candles. On either side of the calabash are hand-woven baskets filled with fruit. A rolled up shawl is carefully placed among them. Just in front of all the items is a small heap of coins. As the hymn continues, individual members of the entourage approach the shrine, say a benediction, and present an offering.

MAPULE, carrying a beret, comes forward and kneels in front of the shrine.

MAPULE

Ousie Dineo, a na o a egopola berete e? Nna ke gopola o e apare, jwale ke go fa yona [My sister Dineo, do you remember this beret? I can still see you wearing it. Now I am giving it to you].

THANDEKA and **SIMANGALISO** kneel in front, side by side, with the bead project. They carefully open the project in dedication to **Dineo**. They stand and **THANDEKA** gently raises **ME'TAU** to join her and **SIMANGALISO**. **MAPULE** then joins the trio. The four women stand in front of the shrine with a sense of accomplishment and closure.

THE END

△▷ Thandeka and Bouda'D remember the farm.

△ The mourning continues.

△ Thandeka and Me'Tau visit Dhlamini's shop.

WE WANT TO
KNOW THE

◁△ Khulumani members on their way to registration.

△▷ Khulumani members at the TRC registration.

△ Thandeka and Me'Tau join the Khulumani members.

REGISTRATION

△ Thandeka and Me'Tau waiting to register.

△ Dineo in flight.

△ Simangaliso in the school corridor.

△ Simangaliso at the cleansing ritual.

△▷ The last moments of Peters' life.

△ Mapule at the ceremony of remembrance.